The Story of the Christian Church
in India and Pakistan

The Story of the Christian Church in India and Pakistan

by

STEPHEN NEILL

WILLIAM B. EERDMANS PUBLISHING COMPANY
GRAND RAPIDS, MICHIGAN

Printed in the United States of America

EDITORIAL FOREWORD

Christian World Mission Books is the name of a library of paperback volumes on all aspects of the world mission of the church of Christ — history, theory, methods, functional approaches, regional studies, biographies, and collections of source material needed by students. These books offer knowledge about the mission to the growing number of historians and general readers who are discovering its importance in cultural interchange and international relations. They are being especially provided as tools for teachers and students in missions and church history, but are equally directed to laymen and pastors in the churches. Sound scholarship underlies each of them, but generally scholarly apparatus is kept at a minimum. Although intended primarily for the American public it is hoped that the books will have wide international distribution and use. The authors have been recruited from many nations and churches. A variety of theological viewpoints are represented, but all writers are personally committed to the mission in some manner. One object of the program is to contribute to dialogue on the fundamentals of missions at a time when there is vigorous debate about the nature, aims, goals, justification, and methods of missions.

This book by Bishop Neill is one in the series "Discipling the Nations," brief histories of the planting and development of churches in several countries and regions through the action of the western churches, and an appraisal of the present

5

state of the indigenous churches in those areas. India is of major importance to the whole missionary enterprise, because the mission there provided models and methods for other fields. Bishop Neill has produced a clear and vivid outline of the story of Christianity in the Indian subcontinent, with simplicity and economy of text, giving an admirable introduction to an exceedingly complex subject. It affords such introduction as is needed by those persons who wish to study in some depth the present situation of Christians in India and Pakistan, and it provides a reliable chart and compass for those who may wish to explore more fully either the whole or aspects of the story of the church in those lands.

R. PIERCE BEAVER
Editor

CONTENTS

Preface   9

   I. The Beginnings   11

  II. Vasco da Gama and All That   27

 III. Protestants Emerge   48

 IV. Free for All   62

  V. Great Days of Colonialism   90

 VI. The Indian Reaction   114

VII. The Growth of Independence   128

VIII. The Church in Independent
      India and Pakistan   155

Bibliography   170

Index   175

PREFACE

To write the history of nineteen centuries in so slim a volume as this is a most difficult and delicate task. If the narrative is too condensed, it becomes completely unreadable. If the principles of selection are influenced by particular interests or by predilection and prejudice, the resulting picture will be distorted and unreliable. I have done my best, by an alternation of rather rapid summary and illustrative incident, to draw a fair and balanced picture of the history of the Indian churches over these many centuries. I hope that I may have been successful in leaving on the mind of the reader a sense of growth, experiment and development, and that I may have put in his hands material which will enable him to form his own judgment as to the present position of the churches in India and Pakistan and as to the problems which they face.

No two writers would make exactly the same selection of material; and I can imagine that some of my readers will be irritated at finding no mention of their favorite mission or of their favorite missionary. Some may be perplexed that there is here hardly a mention of Ceylon or Burma — countries whose history belongs rather to that of southeastern Asia than to that of the Indian subcontinent. I can only plead that I have done my best, and that I have already planned a work on Indian church history on a far more extensive scale, in which I can promise such readers that they will find all the information that they could desire.

One church, the so-called Church of the Thomas Christians, has had a far longer history in India than any other. Two churches only, the Roman Catholic and the Anglican, have spread themselves out, although in places rather thinly, over the whole extent of India and Pakistan. To these three churches, therefore, rather more space has been devoted than to others. Moreover, the Anglicans in India have been privileged to carry through a number of experiments which have been of great significance for the life of all the churches; these have been recorded in some detail. India is one of the oldest of mission fields, and in the history of the church in India we have to deal with almost every problem with which missions in any part of the world have been faced. The influence of the Indian churches, in their strength and in their weaknesses, in their successful experiments and in their failures, has been powerful in many other countries. It is this that makes the study of Indian church history a must for all those who would understand the present position and the future prospects of the churches of Jesus Christ in the last third of the twentieth century.

— STEPHEN NEILL

I

THE BEGINNINGS

THE LAND OF INDIA

THE INDIAN SUBCONTINENT COVERS AN AREA OF MORE THAN ONE and a half million square miles, and carries within it a vast variety of climate and scene. In the far north, Srinagar in Kashmir lies almost on the same latitude as San Francisco, Lisbon or Athens; Cape Comorin, the southernmost point, is only nine degrees north of the equator, and may be compared to Caracas in Venezuela or Addis Ababa in Africa. Some areas in northern India have a somewhat extreme form of continental climate, with temperatures up to 116 Fahrenheit or more in the hot weather, and well below freezing in the brief cold weather; southern India has a fully tropical climate, humid and hot in Kerala, dry and hot in other parts of the Madras Province.

Factors of geography have kept the subcontinent isolated over long periods of time from the rest of the world. The whole northern frontier is guarded for a distance of 2,000 miles by the greatest mountain mass in the world, the Himalayas. Nepal, just to the north of the Indian frontier, contains many of the world's highest mountains. The coastline is long, but unbroken over wide stretches, and even moderately good harbors are few. Some invaders have come in by sea, but far more have come through the difficult land approaches. Where the western Himalayas break down into lower ranges and foothills, there are a number of negotiable passes, as Alexander the Great discovered to his advantage. It has been through the passes of the northwest frontier that the majority of invaders have entered. The history of India is in no small measure the history of its invaders.

Until recently it was thought that Indian history began with the coming of the Aryans, who entered from central Europe or southern Russia sometime in the second millennium B.C. Now, however, we are aware of at least one, possibly several, much earlier civilizations. The greatest discovery so far has been that of the city of Mohenjo-Dāro in Sind, the largest center yet unearthed of the Indus valley civilization.[1] Mohenjo-Dāro is reckoned by the experts to have flourished about the year 2,500 B.C. Evidently it was the home of an advanced and complex way of life. Until the writing found on a number of seals has been deciphered, it will be impossible to do more than speculate as to the relationships and affinities of this civilization, and to guess at the identity of the builders. Links with Sumer have been established with some probability; but it seems that this was a genuinely Indian culture, and not merely an imported and artificial way of living. We do not know when, or in what circumstances, this whole civilization perished without trace.

The Aryan civilization, however, was very different. These invaders brought with them not only their weapons, their horses and their cattle, but also a highly developed form of speech, an older form of the classical Sanskrit. The Rig Veda, a collection of 1,018 hymns, is the oldest classic in any Indo-European language. From it, and from the later Vedic sources, we obtain a rather clear picture of the invaders. They were a vigorous, active and martial race, entirely free from that melancholy by which later generations in India have supposedly been marked. Their chief aim, as set forth

---

[1] Discoveries at Mohenjo-Dāro began as recently as 1922. Up to that date nothing was known of this early civilization.

in their prayers in the Veda, was the accumulation of cattle, and therewith wealth, well-being and respect among their fellows. Their religion was about halfway between that of simple "nature-peoples" and the sophisticated polytheism of later periods. At certain times their gods and goddesses appeared as no more than clearly idealized natural forces; only occasionally was one of these deities as personally identifiable as one of the gods and goddesses of the Olympian pantheon of the Greeks. Images and temples were unknown. But sacrifice was central in their religious scheme. Animal sacrifice was regularly practiced, culminating in the great and picturesque horse sacrifice, which seems to be undoubtedly a substitute for an earlier human sacrifice. Of great importance was Agni, the god of the sacrificial fire, who was at the same time Agni in the heavens (the sun), Agni in the waters (the lightning), and Agni the house-priest, the familiar and welcome guest from the gods among men, to be encountered at the hearth of every man's home. Although there were clear social distinctions between rulers and ruled, there is only one mention, and that in a late book of the Rig Veda, of the institution of caste.

Although to the Hindu the Vedas are inspired revelation, *sruti,* the thing heard, as against *smriti,* the thing remembered or tradition, there is very little of Vedic religion which has maintained itself permanently in Hindu thought or practice, and very little in later Hinduism which can really be traced back to a Vedic origin. After the early period had come to an end, Hindu religion developed in four strikingly different directions.

As the Brahman priesthood gained in influence, ever-increasing importance came to be attached to the sacrifice and to the rituals which accompanied it. The literature in which this ritual tradition is set forth is tedious in the extreme, but contains some striking beginnings of speculation on cosmology and other themes.

In reaction against the aridity of this kind of religion, and perhaps also in reaction on the part of the warrior class against the dominance of the Brahman priesthood, the first beginnings of genuine philosophical speculation appeared among the Hindus. The Upanisads (8th to 5th century B.C.), written mainly in prose, in dialogue form, and with a grace and vivacity which at times almost match the dialogues of Plato, are concerned with the mystery of being, life and death, and the unity of all existence. The concentrated wisdom of the Upanisads can be summed up in the brief phrase *Tat tvam asi*, "that art thou"; the hidden reality of the *Ātman* in man is identical with the hidden *Brahman*, the power by which all things exist and by which they are held together. In this system the all-important person is not the priest but the teacher; salvation is not by sacrifice but by wisdom. Darker shadows, with the development of the idea of *Karma* (retribution) and transmigration, were beginning to fall; but only at certain points is the tone of these ancient writings pessimistic.

Philosophy, like sacrifice, can become arid and lose its saving efficacy. This was the conclusion reached by the young noble Siddhārtha, or Gautama the Buddha (the Awakened One) (c. 563-483 B.C.), when, having for six years sought salvation in vain in the ways of asceticism, he finally reached his own illumination as to the roots of suffering in desire, and as to emancipation from suffering through the extinction of desire. Buddha was the heir of the philosophic tradition, and his revelation too is one of salvation by knowledge. But speculation as to god or gods he sternly rejected. He himself is reported in the tradition to have said, "As in all the oceans there is but one taste, the taste of salt, so in all the teachings there is one taste only, the taste of salvation." And god, if he exists, cannot save, since he also is part of the maze of this perishable existence. Buddhism maintained itself in India for a thousand years, but then began to die out. Its later history belongs to southeast Asia and to the Far East, not to the story of religion in India.[2]

---

[2] In recent years, under the influence of Dr. B. R. Ambedkar, the notable leader of the "Scheduled Castes," there has been a remarkable increase of interest in Buddhism in India. The Census of 1961 recorded 3,250,227 Buddhists in India, or 0.7 per cent of the population.

Gravely threatened by Buddhism, Hinduism recovered through a notable addition to its religious resources. The Bhagavad Gītā, the Lord's Song, best beloved of all Indian classics, is the first great exposition of the religion of *Bhakti*, devoted attachment to a single deity. The tremendous theophany in chapter XI, in which Krishna, the incarnate god who has been serving as the charioteer of the warrior Arjuna, reveals his true nature as the everlasting god, who from time to time, as evil prevails in the earth, becomes incarnate in order to maintain the just and to destroy the unjust, is wholly unlike anything to be found in the earlier Vedic literature, and is scarcely paralleled in Indian literature of later times. The whole of the later history of religion in India has been affected by this little book.[3]

The Aryans, however, were not the only inhabitants of India. The ancient writings are full of tales of their battles with the Dasyus, probably the older and darker inhabitants of northern India, whom in the end they succeeded in reducing to subordination. We have reason to believe that at many points each group strongly influenced the speech and the life of the other. But far in the south, separated from the north by a tangled mass of hill, forest and jungle, lived the Dravidian peoples with their remarkable languages, developing a very different way of life and civilization from the Hindus. In the oldest Tamil romances, which date from the early centuries of the Christian era, we gather a vivid impression of a lively city civilization, supported by extensive commerce, and with a form of religion markedly different from that which we have encountered in the northern regions. It is probably to the Dravidians that later Hinduism owes the temple as the home of a god, the worship of gods in the visible form of idols, and the establishment of *pūjā*, the offering of flowers and the fruits of the earth in place of animal sacrifice. The vigorous Tamil genius eagerly took hold of the concept of *Bhakti*, and set it forth memorably

---

[3] The Bhagavad Gītā has been translated a great many times. A very scholarly and satisfactory edition is that of W. D. P. Hill, with Sanskrit text, prose translation, introduction and commentary.

in Sanskrit prose, and poetically in the Tamil hymns of the
South Indian saints.

WHEN DID THE GOSPEL ARRIVE?

It was to this ancient land, with its already complex and
varied civilizations and its rich religious history, that the
gospel had to be preached. At what stage of development did
the first Christians arrive, and have we any evidence as to
the impression that they made?

In the far southwest of India, isolated between the ocean
and the mountains, lives the most ancient of Indian churches,
the Church of the so-called Thomas Christians. Among these
Christians it is the first article of faith that their church was
founded by the Apostle Thomas, who came in person to
India, and after some years of fruitful ministry died as a
martyr at the hands of Brahmans enraged at the success of
Christian preaching. What estimate should sober history
make of this claim?

There is no *a priori* reason for dismissing the claim as mere
mythology or fantasy. The monsoon wind was discovered in
the first century B.C. Merchants then found that, if they made
use of the southwest wind in certain months of the year
and set their sails and tiller in a particular way, they could
avoid the enormous journey along the coast of Iran and
Baluchistan, and could sail across the open ocean and arrive
much more quickly in India, the land of spices. Landfall
seems usually to have been made in the neighborhood of
Kollam, called Quilon by the Portuguese, but referred to by
medieval writers, irritatingly and confusingly, as Kolumbum.
The northeast wind of the smaller monsoon would then carry
the merchant back to the Red Sea and so home. The discoveries of hoards of Roman coins all over South India, and
still more strikingly of a Roman commercial settlement of
the first century A.D. on the southeast coast of India, at
Arikkamedu in the neighborhood of Pondicherry, make it
clear that commerce between the Roman Empire and South
India was on a grand scale. If Thomas was at any time in
Egypt, there was nothing to prevent his taking ship and

transporting himself to India. But in historical research there is a long gap between possibility and probability, and between probability and virtual certainty. There is really no evidence in favor of the foundation of Indian Christianity by Thomas except the persistent strength of the tradition. Unless further archaeological evidence confirms the tradition, the critical historian must leave the matter with a simple "We do not know."[4]

The first literary evidence for a connection between Thomas and India comes to us from the charming but heretical *Acts of Thomas,* a work of the third century. Here we read that, in the division of the world among the apostles, India fell to the lot of Thomas. This apostle, however, declared that he, a man of Israel, could not go to preach the gospel among Indians whose language he did not know. The Lord then arranged for Thomas, who was a skilled carpenter, to be sold as a slave to one Abbanes, an agent of Gundaphorus, king of India, who was in Jerusalem looking for skilled craftsmen. Much is told of the adventures of Thomas in India, and of course of the miraculous conversion of the king. Scholars had tended to treat all this as mere romance; but the discovery in northwest India of coins of a certain King Gundobar, who must have reigned in the second half of the first century A.D., suggested that at least some facts must lie behind the romance. Clearly there was some connection between Persia and India over the passes, and the writer of the *Acts* may well have had some knowledge of the presence of Christians in India at that early date. But these Christians must have lived in what is now the Punjab, nowhere near the Kerala of the Church of the Thomas Christians.

Our next evidence is a work called *Christian Topography,* by Cosmas Indicopleustes, perhaps the least intelligent of all Greek writers, who had actually made the journey to India, as his name implies, between A.D. 525 and 530; but he tells us hardly anything of what he saw. He does, however,

---

4 The evidence for commerce between the Roman Empire and India is set out by Sir Mortimer Wheeler in *Rome beyond the Imperial Frontiers,* pp. 155-157 and 164-182.

speak plainly of the presence of Christians in South India
and Ceylon. He reports,

> ... in the island of Taprobane (Ceylon) ... there is a church
> with clergy and a congregation of Christians ... and such
> is also the case in the land called Male where the pepper
> grows. ... The island hath also a church of Persian Chris-
> tians who have settled there, and a presbyter who is appointed
> from Persia, and all the apparatus of public worship. But
> the natives and their kings are heathen.

Some important deductions can be made from these few
words of Cosmas. He tells us not of an indigenous Indian
church but of a community of strangers from Persia. The
reference to pepper makes it plain who these strangers were;
they were spice merchants, engaged in the flourishing commerce between India and the Roman Empire. Spices have
played an enormously important part in the history of the
world; the successful pepper merchant was likely to become a
very rich man. It is significant too that the clergy were nomi-
nated from Persia. The links of these remote Christians were
with the Patriarch of Babylon, and this means that although
their descendants claim to have maintained the faith unadul-
terated as transmitted to them by Thomas, they were in fact,
according to Western textbooks, affiliated with the Nestorian
heresy.

This picture of a group of foreign merchants who brought
their faith with them is strongly confirmed by the remarkable evidence of five copper plates, on which are recorded the
privileges granted by one of the local kings to the community
of Christians and to some other groups. There is considerable
doubt as to the actual date of these grants, but the consensus
of opinion seems to fix them at about A.D. 800. These plates
are written in the old Tamil script, but the signatures of
witnesses include a number in Pahlavi (middle Persian),
Arabic in Kufic characters, and a kind of Persian in Hebrew
characters. The king assigns to the church in Quilon a
number of slaves, and at the same time commits to the
Christians the administration of customs, the care of weights
and measures, and probably custody of the official seal. Once

again we notice the presence of strangers and foreigners. But
we see something of the process by which an alien community
became deeply rooted in Indian soil, and came to feel itself
to be part of the Indian people. Doubtless the slaves of the
"Company" were baptized. The traders who settled down
permanently, having come without their wives, married Indian women, and thus the original Persian element dimin-
ished as the percentage of Indian blood increased. This
community, however, although it was prepared to accept
many Hindu customs and ideas, was not prepared to allow
itself to be wholly absorbed by the Hindu majority. It re-
tained its sense of foreignness, and emphasized it at two
points. For centuries the bishop came from the original
homeland of the church; as far as we know, no one born in
India was consecrated to the episcopate until the seventeenth
century. And divine service was always conducted in Syriac
and never in the language of South India. As time passed
the people understood less and less of the Syriac service, and
even among the priests many could do little more than
recite the venerable words. But every Sunday reminded the
worshippers that their spiritual ancestors had come from far
away, and that they were part of a great community other
than that Hindu fellowship that surrounded and so greatly
outnumbered them. It is not for nothing that this community
has been known until the present day as the "Syrians." Not
one in a hundred of the "Syrians" has ever seen Syria; but
they manage to combine in an attractive way complete Indian-
ness with a certain aloofness, as of those who belong also
to another and very different world.

We must end this section by referring briefly to the last of
the strange and moving evidences that have come down to us
from ancient times. In 1547 the Portuguese dug up in the
neighborhood of Madras an ancient stone cross with an
inscription in an unknown tongue. Subsequently three other
similar crosses were discovered, but all appear to be copies
from the original cross discovered in 1547. The unknown
tongue was later identified as Pahlavi (middle Persian), and
a number of attempts have been made by scholars to decipher

and interpret the inscriptions. These remarkably varied interpretations had only one characteristic in common — that none of them agreed in any single point with any of the others. At last the matter was settled by a Cambridge scholar, Dr. Winckworth, who in 1928 produced a translation which in all essentials has been generally accepted as reliable: "My Lord Christ, have mercy on Afras, son of Chaharbukt the Syrian, who cut this." Now this is interesting. There is a considerable weight of tradition concerning a new group of immigrants who came to Quilon in about the year 825, and settled there. Among them were two prelates, Mar Sapor and Mar Aphroth. (The names are also given as Xabro and Prod.) It is just possible that the Afras of the cross and the Mar Aphroth of tradition are one and the same person; if so, the original cross must have come to South India at the beginning of the ninth century, the copies having been cut at later dates. The experts in palaeography would have nothing to say against this dating.

HIDDEN YEARS

We know all too little of this remarkable Christian community during the first five or six hundred years of its existence, though legend is ready and willing to fill out the thin outline of evidence with a thick covering of fantasy. For the next seven hundred years our information is even more fragmentary. For this there is a simple reason. The prophet Muhammad made his famous departure from Mecca to Medina in the year 622 A.D. Within two hundred years his followers had made themselves masters on land and sea. The Muslims controlled the oceans; contact between Europe and the East was reduced to a minimum. Free access was not to be recovered till seven centuries had passed. In the meantime, the church in South India was cut off from almost every form of contact with the outside world.

Yet the cutting off of communication was never absolute. Hardy travelers did from time to time penetrate the unknown lands of India, and brought back with them to Europe tales of what they had seen. Some of their letters and records have been preserved, and give us tantalizing glimpses of a church about which we would like to know so much more. If so much has survived, it is certain that much more has perished, and that the veil of silence was more often broken than we might have been inclined to infer from the small surviving fragments.

New life came into Roman Catholic missionary effort with the foundation of the Franciscan and Dominican Orders in the first half of the thirteenth century, and with the formation about the year 1300 of the *Societas Fratrum Peregrinantium propter Christum inter Gentes,* which directed and guided a new wave of missionary enterprise in the eastern countries. Most of the travelers who enter our story at this point belong to one or the other of these orders.

The first of the great travelers was Marco Polo, who on his way to China spent a considerable time in India, and has included in his account of his travels some vivid pictures of the India of his day. He visited the place near Madras where the body of Thomas was supposed to lie buried. He records that the place, though of no importance commercially, was visited by pilgrims, both Christian and Muslim, and that the Christians living there supported themselves by cultivating the coconut palm. He traveled as far as Quilon, where he also found a small number of Christians.

Next on the list is one of the most remarkable missionaries of medieval times. Inspired by the hope of the conversion to Christianity of the Great Khan, the Pope in 1289 chose as his emissary John of Monte Corvino, who had already had some experience of working in Asia. Unlike the majority of travelers, who went by land across the vast spaces of central Asia, John chose the southern route, and spent thirteen months in India on the way. He was an accurate and intelligent observer. It is unfortunate that only three letters in which he has anything to tell about India have been preserved. He too had visited the Church of the Thomas Christians, and while there had baptized about one hundred persons. He does not tell us who these people were, whether members of the church who in the absence of priests had never been able to be baptized, converts from Hinduism, or Nestorians, whom he regarded as not having been properly baptized. After his stay in India John was able to make his way to Khanbalik (Peking), to reside there for many years, and to obtain consecration as the first Roman Catholic archbishop in the Far East. But this later work falls outside the limits of our present theme.

A few years later, in 1321, another mission reached India, also with the intention of proceeding to China. A French Dominican, Jourdain Catalini de Sévérac, commonly known as Brother Jordan, was traveling in the company of four Franciscans. They landed on the island of Salsette, and there found fifteen families of Nestorian Christians. Jordan crossed to the mainland, leaving the Franciscans at Salsette. During his absence, three of the friars were called before the *Cadi*, the Muslim judge, in connection with a case which had nothing to do with religion. In the course of the inquiry, the judge began to ask them questions about their religion, and at a certain point pressed them for their opinion of Muhammad. One of the brothers, truthfully but imprudently, replied that it was his opinion that Muhammad was the son of perdition and that he was now in hell where the adherents of his religion would follow him in due course. Naturally the fanatical Muslims were enraged. The brothers were tortured and then deported to the mainland, but during the following night they were pursued by armed men and put to death. The one remaining friar was also arrested, tortured and finally beheaded. Jordan heard the news some days later, returned to Salsette, and was allowed to collect the remains of the martyrs and to carry them to a place named Sefa, where there was also a church, for safe Christian burial.[5]

There seems no reason to doubt the accuracy of the story as told by Jordan. It seems that we here have the first reliable record of Christians meeting their death at the hands of Indians by reason of their faith. The story is also important, as it gives us evidence of a much wider distribution of Chris-

---

[5] See John Foster, "The Four Martyrs of Thana 1321," *International Review of Missions*, XLVI (1956), 204-208.

tians in India than we might otherwise have inferred from our records. Jordan himself remained in India, writing somewhat bitterly of the hardships he 'had endured at the hands of the inhabitants, but holding out good hope of great results, if there could be in India "but two or three hundred good friars, who could preach faithfully and fervently the Catholic faith." Of the Nestorians he formed a very poor opinion; they are, he says, "a scattered people, one here, another there, who call themselves Christians but are not so, nor do they have baptism, nor do they know anything about the faith; nay, they believe St. Thomas the Great to be Christ." It must not be forgotten that visitors like Jordan were dependent on often unsatisfactory interpreters, and also that his mind was clearly full of medieval Western prejudice against all Christians of other traditions. What he writes may have been true of some of the small groups which he encountered in different parts of the country, but it can hardly be supposed that his statements would be found accurate if applied to the main body of the Thomas Christians in Travancore.

Our next witness to the state of Christianity in India is the oddest of all. John de Marignolli had spent a considerable time in India around the year 1348. On his return to Europe, he was taken up by the Emperor and given the tedious task of writing the chronicles of Bohemia. At a certain point, overwhelmed by the tedium of his task of writing this very boring chronicle, John diverged from his appointed task and inserted into his chronicle a rather lively account of his experiences in India. Five centuries later, some industrious bookworm, undeterred by weariness, read the chronicles and found in them unexpectedly this firsthand information about medieval India. Since that time John has found his place in every account of the Christian church in India. Marignolli deserves this place in the records, since what he has to say is of considerable interest. He tells us that on Palm Sunday, 1348, he and his companions arrived at a very noble city of India called Quilon, where the whole world's pepper is produced. And the Saracens (Muslims) were not the proprietors of the trade but the Thomas Christians. There was a church of St. George of the Latin rite in the city, and there Marignolli lived for a while and taught the holy law. He erected there a memorial pillar, and after fourteen months of residence left this agreeable city.

Marignolli's relations with the Thomas Christians seem to have been pleasant and friendly. Perplexing is his note on a Christian church of the Latin rite in the city. He cannot have been mistaken; but here again we have one of those detached notices, which lead us to surmise a more extensive presence of Christianity in India than we had been inclined to allow for. This church must have been erected by Italian traders, from Genoa or Pisa or possibly Venice. The Italians, who were passionately eager merchants, were inclined to maintain friendly relations with the Muslim powers; it appears that at a time at which the other European powers were locked in desperate conflict with the Muslims, at least some of the Italian republics had managed to open a way to India and to secure their share of the immensely profitable trade in those spices which Europe simply could not do without.

Here we must bring to a conclusion our brief survey of these dark centuries. What we have learned, beyond all shadow of doubt, is that, weak and helpless as the church may have been in India, it continued to exist, to maintain itself against all tendencies to syncretism and absorption, and was there to be welcomed with surprise and delight when at last Europe found its way back to the Asian world.

CHRISTIAN INFLUENCE ON INDIA

We have admitted that in many ways Christians in India were influenced by the point of view and the practices of the non-Christians by whom they were surrounded. It is natural to ask whether the presence of the Christian church exercised any notable influence on India and the religions of the country.

Some scholars, eager to claim all excellence for Christ Jesus, have attempted to see clear traces of a widespread influence of the Christian gospel on the higher levels of Hindu thought and practice. For instance, some who have been deeply impressed by the doctrine of divine love and of man's love for God in the Bhagavad Gītā, have thought that that great poem must be post-Christian, and that some of the almost Johannine phrases that are to be found in it must be due to a direct influence of the gospel upon the writer. But this view has now been abandoned by all serious Indologists. The idea of the love of God, though it may in Christianity have reached heights hitherto unknown, is not wholly absent from the other religions of the world. It is almost certain that the doctrine of *Bhakti,* as set forth in the Gītā, grew up on Indian soil without influence from any other source.

The great Tamil scholar G. U. Pope was profoundly impressed by the ethical quality of the *Tirukurral,* the greatest of all Tamil classics, which was probably composed in the second century A.D.; he was inclined to think that Christian influences played a part in the composition of this great work: "I cannot feel any hesitation in saying that the Christian Scriptures were among the sources from which the poet derived his inspiration." He draws a pleasing picture of Tiruvalluvar pacing along the seashore with the Christian teachers, and "imbibing Christian ideas, tinged with the peculiarities of the Alexandrian school, and day by day working them into his own wonderful *Kurral.*"[6] It is sad to have to say that such pictures belong to the realm of pure fantasy. The *Kurral* is certainly among the greatest of non-Christian classics. Its jeweled couplets are learned by heart by every pupil in every school in the Tamil country, and the mind of the Tamil people has been penetrated by its splendidly high ethical teaching, so much so that the Tamils have a more acute sense of right and wrong than any other Indian people. But if we hold that this noble contribution to human literature and thought is in some way dependent on the living Christ, we must think rather of the *logos spermatikos* of Justin Martyr, that Word of God which sows seeds by the wayside among the sons of men. Some of these seeds may grow up and give evidence of a work of God in the world

---

[6] G. U. Pope, *The Tirukurral,* p. xviii.

wider than can be expressed in purely Christian categories. But there is no reason to suppose that the great poet of the Tamil south had been exposed to direct Christian influences.

The more we study this long Christian history, the more we receive the impression of an isolated folk, influenced by their surroundings but exercising little influence upon them. The main body of Christians, the Thomas Christians, were remote in their little area between the mountains and the sea. They never traveled beyond it, and did not exercise any Christian influence beyond the immediate neighborhood in which they lived. Other communities were too small and feeble to do more than exist through the centuries of darkness. It is one of the miracles of church history that these churches did continue to exist, so isolated, so threatened, so tempted by every possibility of betrayal of their Christian substance. But the day of their great awakening did not come until new and in some ways destructive influences from without were brought to bear upon them. Indian Christianity was destined to become fully alive only after it had been exposed to confrontation with the more developed Christianity of the West.

II

VASCO DA GAMA AND ALL THAT

A NEW BEGINNING IN HISTORY

TWO EVENTS, ONE AT THE END OF THE FIFTEENTH CENTURY, the other some time later in the sixteenth, permanently changed the entire face of the history of India. In the summer of 1498 the three small ships of Vasco da Gama cast anchor in the roadstead off Calicut in southwest India. On April 21, 1526, the Mongol invader from central Asia, Bābur, at the battle of Panipat made himself master of northwest India.

As we have seen, India has always been accessible to invaders entering by the difficult but not impossible passes of the northwest. Bābur, who was not only a highly competent soldier but also a gifted and cultivated man, had been on the frontier since 1505, but made his advance cautiously and gradually into India. The decisive battle took place about fifty miles north of Delhi, when Bābur's small army utterly defeated the far larger host of Sultan Ibrahim. As he piously recorded in his memoirs, "By the grace and mercy of almighty God, this difficult affair was made easy for me, and that mighty army in the space of half a day was laid in the dust."[1]

---

1 Quoted from Bābur's *Memoirs* in R. C. Majumdar, H. C. Raychaudhuri and K. Datta, *An Advanced History of India*, p. 427.

The firm foundation of the Mogul empire in India had been laid.

Except for one brief century under British rule, the Indian subcontinent has never been a political unity. The Moguls, however, in the two centuries of their effective rule, came nearer than any other power to bringing about such unity. They produced a number of able rulers, and one, Akbar, must be accounted one of the greatest rulers that the world has ever known. Themselves Muslims, the Moguls were tolerant of other faiths and did their utmost to promote the welfare of all kinds of men. Their rule, though autocratic, was never harsh, and justice was on the whole well administered throughout their wide realms. It was with this great empire that the new arrivals from Europe had to deal.

From the tenth century onwards the Muslims had been in control of the seas, and Europe was almost wholly cut off from Asia and the East. The old trade routes both by land and sea were closed, and Europe had no direct access to the spices and other treasures of the Asian lands. As European power began to recover, attempts were constantly being made to circumvent the Muslim powers, and to find new sea routes lying outside their control. When Columbus touched land west of the Atlantic, he believed himself to have reached India — hence the name "Indian" still borne by the aboriginal inhabitants of the Western world. Under the direction of Prince Henry the Navigator, Portuguese sailors had been pressing ever further south in the belief that somewhere Africa must end, and that a sea way to Asia must become accessible. In 1487 Bartholomew Diaz showed that this conjecture was well founded. Eleven years later Vasco da Gama launched out on the waters of the Indian Ocean, and the long-sought goal was attained.

The one object of the Portuguese was trade. They had no thought of founding in the East such a great empire as they had acquired in Brazil, since the available resources would have been far too slender for any such undertaking. All they required was the possession of a small number of strong points, based on which their fleets could chase the Muslims

off the seas, and their traders could open up commerce with
the hinterland. In 1510 Albuquerque, the ablest of the
Portuguese viceroys in the East, captured the city of Goa and
the adjoining territory. To this were added settlements at
Cochin in the southwest, Tuticorin and Mylapore in the
southeast, and the great port of Malacca in what is now
Malaya.

LIFE IN THE PORTUGUESE CITIES

It was the aim of the Portuguese to reproduce in India as
closely as possible the life to which they were accustomed
at home. Goa soon emerged as a city of palaces and great
churches, and several of the great Roman Catholic Orders
were represented in its convents. The Portuguese felt no
strong impulse to preach the gospel to the people of India
as a whole. Nor, as is often affirmed, did they exercise force to
bring the local inhabitants to the Christian faith. It was,
however, firmly held that idolatry must not be practiced in
the territories of a Christian king; if the people wished to
retain their disagreeable rites, they must observe them secretly
and out of sight. No doubt many inducements were held
out to the Hindus with a view to securing their assent to the
new faith; a non-Christian could hardly hope for employment or advancement under this Christian government. But
those who accepted the Christian faith were always a minority
of the inhabitants.[2]

One fruitful source of conversion was mixed marriages.
The European men always far outnumbered the women.
Albuquerque, making a virtue of necessity, strongly urged
his soldiers to marry the "white and beautiful" widows and
daughters of those Muslims who had fallen in defense of Goa,
thus both strengthening their own attachment to a country
from which they were unlikely to return to Europe, and also
increasing the population upon which the authorities would
be able to rely in time of trouble. From such unions arose

---

[2] The Jesuits always conscientiously recorded the exact number of baptisms; and they were surprisingly small, as shown in Fr. J. Wicki's splendid
series, *Documenta Indica* (to date 11 vols.).

many of the most distinguished families of Goa, as strongly Roman Catholic today as four centuries ago. There were also many casual and illicit relationships. The offspring of such unions were generally baptized; but little was done for them, and, as often happens in such circumstances, a mixed population began to grow up which seemed to manifest the worst characteristics of both the races from which it was derived.

FRANCIS XAVIER AND THE JESUITS

The whole situation changed for the better with the arrival in Goa in 1542 of Francis Xavier (1506-52), one of the first companions of Ignatius Loyola in the formation of the Society of Jesus, and one of the outstanding missionaries of all times. Xavier had come out, not as an ordinary missionary, but as the friend and correspondent of the king of Portugal, armed also with considerable powers by the Pope for oversight and control of all missions in the Far East. He spent in all little more than four years in India, but at a number of points his work was decisive for the whole future of the Indian church.

His first task was to attempt to bring some sort of order into the church life of Goa, and here his eager pastoral heart found satisfaction, especially in work among the children. But this was not the task that he had come to the East to do; it was not long before he began the travels which were to occupy him for the rest of his life. The first call for wider activity came from the Coromandel Coast, the long strip of land lying between Madras and Cape Comorin.

The fisher folk of this area, a rough and hardy caste commonly known as the Paravas, or as they prefer to call themselves, the Bharathas, had been suffering endlessly from the raids of pirates and land-raiders from the north. Hearing of the new power that had appeared in India, they desired to place themselves under the protection of the foreigners. Their request was granted, on the condition that they accept baptism and regard the king of Portugal as their overlord. The terms were accepted. In a brief space the entire caste, numbering perhaps ten thousand people, was baptized, without any instruction and with no provision for spiritual care; all that the people knew was that they were now called Christians. There is some doubt as to the date at which these events took place. The most probable date seems to be 1536, or six years before the arrival of Xavier in Goa. During these years nothing had been done for these people, except that the strong arm of Portuguese protection had made it possible for them to live.

As soon as affairs in Goa had been brought into order, Xavier set out to seek in person the lost sheep. The task which lay before him was formidable. The Paravas lived scattered in small villages along two hundred miles of the coast. They managed their catamarans with extraordinary skill and hardihood. Income from their craft, though not large, was steady, and they were by no means the poorest in the land. But their rough life had given them little opportunity to acquire the amenities of civilization; they were untouched by the higher elements of Hindu culture, and they were illiterate almost to a man.

Xavier's letters give a vivid and attractive picture of his attempts to create something like an orderly church out of this chaos. Later legend has attributed to him a miraculous gift of tongues. The evidence of his own letters makes it clear that this legend rests on no foundation whatsoever, that Xavier never managed to acquire more than the rudiments of the difficult Tamil language, and that he was dependent on interpreters whose competence left very much to be desired. His first activity, after making initial contacts with the people, was to hammer out, with such help as he could secure, rough translations of the Lord's Prayer, the Apostles' Creed, the Ten Commandments and some other prayers. Later study showed that these translations were in fact very rough and at certain points misleading, but at least a beginning had been made. The children were used as the focus of instruction, but older people as well were gathered regularly for worship. Xavier worked out an excellent form of catechetical instruction, involving a great deal of repetition of the essential texts, with responses which the people could easily learn by heart:

> On Sunday I assemble all the people, men and women, young and old. . . . I give out the first commandment, which they repeat, and then we say all together, Jesus Christ, Son of God, grant us grace to love thee above all things. When we have asked for this grace, we recite the Paternoster together, and then cry with one accord, Holy Mary, Mother of Jesus Christ, obtain for us grace from thy Son to enable us to keep the first commandment . . . and so on through all the other commandments.

Xavier's greatest problem was the incompetence of his assistants. It was not his intention to stay long on the Fisher Coast. He had given to the people the gift of his burning zeal and his intense love of souls. He would never be forgotten, and even the thick veil of tasteless and trivial legend would not be able to conceal the real greatness of the man and his work. But what was to come after him? There were few Jesuit priests in India. The College of St. Paul had been founded at Goa to train students for the ministry from all the Indian races; but this work was only in its beginnings, and by no means all of the students enrolled in it were proving satisfactory. It seemed not unlikely that when Xavier passed on to his greater work of the evangelization of Japan, everything that he had done on the Fisher Coast might simply collapse.

As later events were to show, Xavier had no need to be anxious. The little company of the friends of Loyola grew with astonishing rapidity and before long became a great missionary army. India was one of the favored mission fields. By the end of the sixteenth century the Jesuits had succeeded in gathering the Christians together in sixteen large villages, in each of which a Jesuit priest was resident. The priest exercised a wide-reaching and paternal authority over every part of the life of the people. It was a strict rule that there must be no fishing on Sunday, and that part of every Friday's catch must be handed over for the support of the church. Little was done for education, and as in Portugal itself the greater part of the population remained illiterate. But gradually the life and mind of the people came to be saturated with the Roman Catholic tradition as it had developed in the days after the Council of Trent. The Fisher Coast is still an almost entirely Roman Catholic country.

The work of Xavier resulted in resounding success, but the limitations of this method must also be noted. The entire caste of the Paravas had become Christian; there were therefore no dissenters and none of the painful schisms within groups and families which we shall have to take note of in other areas. But the conversion of this caste had no direct effect whatsoever on any other group in the neighborhood. The Parava Christians were so completely encapsulated by the caste system that they existed for themselves alone. To some extent they were under the influence of the neighboring Hindus, whose great temples in such cities as Tiruchendur towered over them, but they themselves exercised no Christian influence, as far as can be detected, on those with whom they had no other than business relationships.[3] Caste divisions were then, as now, the gravest problem with which Christian missions in India have had to deal.

ROME AND THE THOMAS CHRISTIANS

It was not long before the Portuguese discovered the existence of the ancient Church of the Thomas Christians, for the survival of which we have seen evidence from time to time throughout the middle ages. The Portuguese strong point at Cochin was in the close neighborhood of Angamalle, one of the chief centers of the Thomas Christians; and the whole of the Serra (mountains) through which they were scattered was easily accessible to European visitors. Both parties were delighted with the discovery. The Portuguese were surprised and pleased to find possible Christian allies in this strange

---

[3] The first Jesuit permanently settled on the coast, Fr. Henry Henriquez, does record his disputations with Hindus, and an occasional conversion; but the contacts were few, and seem to have become fewer as the Paravas increasingly settled down to live as a Christian people. An example is given in a letter of January 12, 1551, in Wicki, *op. cit.,* vol. 2, pp. 157-158.

country. It was affirmed that the Christians numbered 30,000 families, and they could put in the field 30,000 armed men. This figure may be an exaggeration, but at least the Christians could be reckoned as no inconsiderable force. On the other side, the Christians, accustomed to long isolation from the rest of the Christian world and to the difficulties with the local rajahs to which they were constantly exposed, were charmed by the genuine friendship shown to them by many of the Portuguese, and by the thought that the strong arm of the king of Portugal might be raised in their defense in time of need.

There were from the start, however, certain difficulties in the situation. The links of the Thomas Christians were all with Mesopotamia, from which they had invariably received their bishops. They had never heard of the Pope and were incensed at being accused of Nestorian heresy, being themselves convinced that they had maintained uncontaminated the true faith as they had received it from their founder, the Apostle Thomas. To certain Western customs they took grave exception. For instance, though in many points they had assimilated Hindu ways, they had always scrupulously avoided the use of images, this being one of their safeguards against absorption into an idolatrous society. The Roman insistence on statues and images in church seemed to them calculated to reduce Christians to the level of an idolatrous sect. The Westerners, on the other hand, found it very strange that any Christians should refuse to recognize that the bishop of Rome had been appointed by providence as the father of all Christians and the head of all churches.

Relations throughout the sixteenth century were tangled and tortuous. The crisis came in the year 1599. A new archbishop had come to Goa; it was not long before he made up his mind that the matter of the Thomas Christians must be settled once and for all and that he was the man to settle it. At the time of his appointment, Aleixo de Menezes, scion of an aristocratic family, was only thirty-five years old, but he had already held high office in Portugal. He had come to India, imbued with all the ideas of the Counter-reformation

and determined that there must be no doubt as to the sub-
jection of all Christians everywhere to the authority of the
Pope, and of the Thomas Christians in particular to his own
authority as the Pope's representative in the East.

In the autumn of 1598 Menezes took advantage of the
death of the one remaining Syrian bishop, Mar Abraham, to
come down to the Serra, and to put his carefully laid plans
into execution. Doubts have subsequently been raised as to
whether Menezes had any canonical right to act in the way
that he did;[4] he himself was vexed by no doubts at all. It
is stated in a number of sources that Menezes had promised
not to hold any ordinations in the Serra. If he had in fact
given any such promise, he quickly broke it. Noting the intense attachment of the Eastern clergy to the bishop by whom
they had been ordained, he at once announced that he would
hold ordinations; within a short time at least a hundred
young men had been ordained to the priesthood. Menezes
had powerful allies in the Jesuits, who for a number of years
had been running at Vaipicotta a seminary for the training
of candidates for the priesthood. It was also to his advantage
that the Portuguese in Cochin were on his side and stood by
him throughout.

Menezes next proceeded to summon a synod of the entire
church. On June 20, 1599, 153 priests and 660 lay representatives met at Udiyampērūr (Diamper). It was clear that the
Christians had not been called to discuss, but to obey. Decrees
for the reform of the church, some of them necessary and
salutary, others intended simply to replace local by Roman
customs, had been carefully prepared ahead of time, and
were read out day by day to the assembled throng. By June
26 all was over; the decrees had been accepted in their entirety,
and were signed by all present, starting with Menezes himself. The ancient Church of the Thomas Christians, as an
independent church, had simply ceased to exist.[5]

----

[4] This question is discussed in "The Invalidity of the Synod of Diamper," *Indian Church History Review*, I, 1 (1967), 9ff.

[5] An English translation of the Acts and Decrees of the Synod of
Diamper is printed in J. Hough, *Christianity in India*, vol. 2, pp. 513-683.

Menezes returned to Goa, leaving as bishop the learned Jesuit Francis Roz. Roz was personally acceptable to the Christians; but when they learned that he was not to be, as their own bishops had always been, the independent head of their church but only a suffragan of Goa, the arrangement seemed to them to be a very bad one indeed. The Jesuits were often harsh and less than tactful in their administration. Many of the Christians felt a much stronger loyalty to the archdeacon, their own local head, than to the foreign bishop appointed from Rome. The feeling grew steadily stronger that there would be no peace until they were again given an Eastern bishop such as they had always had in the past. In 1652 hope dawned; they heard that a bishop named Ahatalla was on his way to join them. Then came the bad news that Ahatalla had been arrested by the Portuguese and would never be allowed to reach the Serra. At this point the Thomas Christians could endure no more. A great gathering was held before the Koonen cross at Mattancerri; the Thomas Christians swore to expel the Jesuits, and to submit to no ecclesiastical authority other than that of the archdeacon until they should receive a bishop from an Eastern church. At a later meeting on May 22, 1653, the archdeacon was consecrated as bishop by the laying on of the hands of twelve priests, the best form of consecration they could devise in ·the absence of a bishop.

Immediate measures were taken by Rome to stem the tide of disaffection. Spanish Carmelites were sent in to replace the Jesuits. By tactful approaches these new missionaries won back the hearts of many of the Thomas Christians; but the lost unity was never restored. At the end of a period of twenty years, it was found that about two-thirds of the people had remained within the Roman allegiance; one-third stood by the archdeacon and had organized themselves as the independent Malankara Church, faithful to the old Eastern traditions and hostile to all the Roman claims. In all of the

There is reason to think that the Portuguese text printed at Coimbra in 1606 does not correspond exactly to the text as read and accepted at the synod.

subsequent period the lines of division have hardly changed, and things remain much as they were three centuries ago.

THE JESUITS AND THE GREAT MOGUL

In Europe the Jesuits, eagerly set on the recovery of the Protestant world for the Roman Catholic faith, had attained considerable success by the attention they paid to the aristocracy and to the families of rulers. It was natural that they should ask themselves whether similar methods could be used with success in India. They had been able to secure the conversion of one or two minor rajas. Much more exciting prospects seemed to open up before them with the possibility of access to the great Mogul himself.

Akbar, who came to the throne in 1556 and ruled till 1605, was a man of great intelligence and considerable interest in religion. About the year 1575 he became dissatisfied with the Islamic faith in which he had been brought up, and, having heard of the Jesuits at the College of St. Paul in Goa, he asked that a mission might be sent to his court. In 1579 three fathers were dispatched. They were received with great kindness by Akbar, who arranged for public debates between the Jesuits and the Muslim teachers; he himself took pleasure in listening to their discussions. At first the hopes of the Jesuits ran high, but they were acting under a misapprehension. Already the mind of Akbar was turning towards the establishment of his own patent religion, the *Din Illahi,* a synthetic faith which was intended to bring all the subjects of the Mogul empire into unity. At the end of three years it became clear that there was not the least likelihood of the emperor's conversion, and the mission returned to Goa. But Akbar was still unsatisfied and friendly. A second mission was sent in 1590, and a third in 1595. The head of this third mission was Jerome Xavier, a great-nephew of the saint and a highly skilled disputant; he was at the court of the great Mogul almost continuously from 1595 till 1615.

At times hope soared up again. In 1601 Akbar made it legally possible for his subjects to accept the Christian faith.

His successor Jehangir was outstandingly friendly. He permitted three of his nephews to be instructed and baptized, and the influence of the Jesuits on the ladies of the royal house was considerable. This was the high point of the mission. Jehangir died in 1627, and his successors were fiercely Muslim. Converts were very few and difficulties many. Although some form of mission was maintained until well into the eighteenth century, the Jesuit fathers increasingly became chaplains to Armenian and other Christians about the court, and the hope of any extensive conversion of Hindus and Muslims died away. This was not to be the path along which the gospel would find its way into the heart of India.

THE MADURA MISSION

The sixteenth century in India had been a time of ups and downs for Roman Catholic missions; the seventeenth was to be distinguished by one of the most remarkable undertakings in the whole history of the Christian church.

In 1606 an Italian Jesuit, Robert de Nobili, after a short period of training on the Fisher Coast, arrived in the great city of Madura, the center of Tamil culture in South India. He was distressed to find that the Portuguese custom of Europeanizing all Christians had made Christianity so detestable in the eyes of all respectable Hindus that the conversion of even a single high-caste man was hardly to be expected. De Nobili decided to change all this. In order to win the high-caste Indian he must first himself become an Indian. His first step was to separate himself as far as possible from his Portuguese colleagues in the mission and from the Paravas and other Christians of lower caste. He made a most careful study of Indian usage, and gradually adopted the ways and manners of a Brahman. This meant total vegetarianism, the use of wooden sandals only, leather being forbidden to the higher castes, and of course the adoption of Indian dress. Next, de Nobili set himself to master the Indian languages, and acquired in addition to Tamil and Telugu such a mastery of the classical Sanskrit that he has been described by the great Indologist Max Müller as "our first Sanskrit scholar."

It takes considerable imagination to grasp the measure of sacrifice involved in adopting such a manner of life in that burning climate.

De Nobili's change of method was followed by almost immediate success. India is ever ready to listen to the words of reformers, and it seems that de Nobili was taken to be the head of a Hindu reforming sect. Ere long a number of converts of the highest castes had been baptized. As far as possible de Nobili allowed these converts to retain their old way of living. They were not required to have any contact with Christians of lower caste. They could keep the *kudumi*, the tuft of hair which the Portuguese missionaries had ordered their converts to cut off. They might wear a sacred thread, the sign of the twice-born castes, though this was to be slightly different from that worn by Hindus, and of course was to be put on with Christian prayers and not with Hindu ceremonies. Legend has greatly exaggerated the numbers brought into the church by de Nobili; it appears that in point of fact about 600 persons of the higher castes had been baptized in thirty-seven years, but that not all of these had remained faithful. It was only when the movement spread to the lower castes (not the outcastes) within the Hindu structure that something like a mass movement began to develop.

De Nobili's methods brought on him the fierce hostility of missionaries holding other points of view; it seemed to the more conservative that by his concessions to his converts he was destroying the very essence of Christianity. De Nobili defended himself with great ability, and in 1623 Rome itself pronounced, though somewhat cautiously, in his favor.[6] A century later other counsels prevailed, and all the peculiar usages of the Madura mission were condemned. To many it has seemed that this was a fatal renunciation. It may be

---

[6] The publication at Tuticorin in South India in recent years of a number of de Nobili's Tamil writings makes it plain that in matters of doctrine he was not prepared to make any concessions at all. He remained a rigid controversialist of the Counter-reformation fashion. See D. Yesudhas, "Indigenization or Adaptation?," *Bangalore Theological Forum*, II (1967), 39-52.

thought that de Nobili made many mistakes; it is not clear
that his converts ever understood what they were really
taking on, or recognized that by accepting Christ they were
cutting themselves off forever from the whole tradition of
Hindu life and thought in which they had grown up. But
at least an attempt had been made to domesticate the gospel
in India; now the attempt had been abandoned, and for two
centuries all Roman Catholic missionary effort in India
would consist of the attempt exactly to reproduce on that
foreign soil the details of Roman practice and order.

De Nobili died old and blind in 1656. But the work of
the Madura mission did not cease with the death of the
founder. The missionaries who were able to stand the loneli-
ness and self-denial involved in the course that de Nobili had
marked out for himself were always few — at times there
were no more than six missionaries for the whole area. But
the work continued. It is sufficient in this brief narrative to
take account of only two of the later witnesses.

John de Britto, the son of a viceroy of Brazil, came to
India in 1673. At that time the attitude of the authorities
towards Christians was less favorable than it had been earlier.
De Britto's special concern was with the Christians in the
area now known as Ramnad. For seven years the opposition
of the local ruler had made it impossible for any Jesuit to visit
the scattered Christians. De Britto's first visit, in 1686, ended
in imprisonment and torture, but in the end he and his companions were set free by the local ruler. With undiminished
confidence de Britto attempted a second visit in 1693; this
time no release was made; the Jesuit was beheaded outside
the little town of Uraiyur, leaving behind the memory of a
singularly guileless and gentle personality and of total devotion to the cause of Christ.

Very different in character and manner of living was Constantius Joseph Beschi, an Italian who came to India in 1700
and worked in the mission of Madura till 1742. Beschi
adopted all the ways and manners of the Hindu *Guru* or religious teacher not without a good deal of the arrogance
often found in the members of that class. What distinguished

him from his fellows was his astonishing mastery of the Tamil language. The learned Dr. G. U. Pope refers to him as the greatest of European Tamil scholars. His longest and most famous work, the *Tēmbāvani* or *Unfading Garland,* which is about the same length as the *Odyssey* and is a diffuse and unmethodical setting forth of the gospel story, is so completely Tamil in the manner of its expression that it has been accepted by Indian scholars as one of the classics of the language. No other European has ever attained such eminence in this field of literary excellence. Beschi had to face the problem of the to him extremely unwelcome arrival of the Lutheran missionaries in 1706. He was unsparing in his criticism of their ways and work, their use of the Tamil language and their ignorance of the realities of Indian life. He has left behind an amusing satire, in which he proves to his own satisfaction that the Lutherans are the locusts of Revelation 9; this document was republished well on in the nineteenth century as anti-Protestant propaganda on the part of Roman Catholics in South India.

South India was the specially chosen field of the Jesuits, but we must not suppose that this was their only area of enterprise. For a number of years they maintained a mission on the borders of Tibet, a land that the Christian gospel has never managed to penetrate. And one of their number, Bento de Goes, a native of the Azores, set out in 1603 from Lahore to traverse the vast wastes of central Asia in an attempt to ascertain whether the Cathay of Marco Polo was the same as the China of more recent travelers. De Goes did indeed reach the confines of China in 1607, but there he died, having just managed to establish contact with Matthew Ricci and the flourishing Jesuit mission of Peking.

THE SECULARS ENTER THE FIELD

The early missionaries of the Roman Catholic Church, in the period of the great discoveries and after, had almost all been members of one or other of the religious orders. The Jesuits were the most prominent, but Augustinians, Franciscans and Dominicans also played a notable part. These orders enjoyed various exemptions, and for the most part worked without episcopal supervision. In all his years in the Far East Francis Xavier rarely, if ever, saw a bishop. A great change took place in the seventeenth century with the organization in Rome in 1622 of the Sacred Congregation for the Propagation of the Faith. The first secretary of the Propaganda, as it is generally called, Francesco Ingoli, who held office for more than a quarter of a century, had three aims: to see that Rome was kept constantly informed of all that was happening in the missions, to extend the missionary episcopate, and to bring the secular clergy into the work which had so far been almost an exclusive preserve of the religious orders.

To the extension of the episcopate in the East there was one grave obstacle. In the fifteenth century the Pope had given to the king of Portugal exclusive right, under the system called the *Padroado,* to create bishoprics, and to nominate and support bishops and other missionaries. A number of bishoprics had been created, the most notable being Goa. But again and again bishoprics were left without bishops for long periods; it became increasingly clear that Portugal, a country with less than a million inhabitants, could find neither the men nor the funds for the maintenance of this vast enterprise. Yet the rulers of Portugal were tenacious in maintaining their claims, and in refusing to recognize the right of Rome to appoint bishops for areas not directly under Portuguese jurisdiction.

Ingoli's provisional solution was the appointment of Vicars Apostolic, direct representatives of the Pope in episcopal orders, whose territorial titles would be derived not from the area in which they were actually going to work, but from some see *in partibus infidelium,* with which they could have no more than nominal connection. One of the most imaginative of the measures taken by Ingoli was the consecration in 1637 of a young Brahman convert from the neighborhood of Goa, Matthew de Castro. The original idea was that Matthew should go to Ethiopia; when this proved impossible he was sent back to India to work among his own people. At once difficulties arose. Matthew had an insuperable dislike for Portuguese and Jesuits; he went out to India determined, as he himself expressed it, "to give those Paulists hell" (so he described the Jesuits from the College of St. Paul in Goa). Their dislike of him was if anything greater than his dislike of them. Since he had not been appointed by the king of Portugal, the archbishop of Goa refused to recognize him as validly consecrated or appointed. Eventually the tensions became so strong that in 1658 Matthew was recalled to Rome. He lived on till 1677, apparently liked and respected in Rome, but played no further part in Indian ecclesiastical history. After this first less than fortunate experiment, Rome became very cautious in the matter of an Asian episcopate; two centuries and more were to pass before Indians in any numbers were raised to the episcopal dignity.

The first missionaries, as we have seen, had been mainly Portuguese, though the English Jesuit Thomas Stevens deserves mention. This remarkable man, who is, as far as we know, the only Jesuit of his race to serve the missionary cause in India in the early period, arrived in the country in 1579, and spent the rest of a long life in the mission in western India. He made himself a master of the Konkani language, and left behind him an immense *purāna* (historical composition) in that language, in which the story of the Old Testament and of the Gospels was set out in metrical form, but in a style not too difficult for ordinary people to understand.[7]

A new factor entered the Indian situation when France became the great source of missionaries. In 1663, the *Société des Missions Etrangères* (Society for Missions Overseas) founded a seminary in Paris for the training of those who would go to work in the missions. Ten years later the French colony of Pondicherry was founded on the southeast coast of India, not far from the main centers of the Jesuit enter-

---

[7] A letter written by Thomas Stevens to his father immediately after his arrival in Goa on October 24, 1579, is printed by J. C. Locke, *The First Englishmen in India*, pp. 18-31. Stevens notes that "The drink of this country is good water, or wine of the Palm tree, or of a fruit called Cocos." Stevens died in 1619.

prise. Originally the French, like everyone else from the West, came to trade and for no other purpose. Later on, Pondicherry became the center of vast political ambitions, to which we shall have to refer in another context. At first it was no more than a comparatively small market town, far less splendid than Goa or Cochin. But the presence of an alien power in the midst of what it regarded as its own area, and the incursion of secular priests into a field which had so far been cultivated only by members of the religious orders, and of priests who owed allegiance to their own Vicar Apostolic sent out from Rome without reference to the king of Portugal, could not but be extremely disagreeable to the Jesuit authorities. The expansion of the work of the *Société* was not rapid; but a principle had been introduced which was to be of capital importance in the nineteenth century.

DAYS OF DECLINE

The eighteenth century did not fulfill for the Portuguese the brilliant promise of the seventeenth. The resources of Portugal became ever more strained in Europe. In the East the challenge of the Protestant powers was increasingly felt. As early as 1633 the Dutch had captured Cochin, and proceeded to establish their authority over areas which had been regarded by the Portuguese as their exclusive possession. Missionary interest in Europe seemed to be dying down, and it was not always possible to replace missionaries who had died or had returned to their homeland.

A heavy blow was dealt to Jesuit methods and Jesuit practice by the arrival in India of a special legate of the Pope, Charles Maillard de Tournon, specially commissioned to settle the question of the adaptation of Christian rites to Indian and Chinese custom, which had been permitted by the Jesuits but harshly criticized by the other orders. Tournon, who reached Pondicherry in 1704, decreed at every point in condemnation of Jesuit practice. In all matters of ritual and custom, all must be carried out exactly according to the rules of Rome as these had developed since the Counter-reformation. Those features of the Roman baptismal rite, such as the use of salt and spittle, which were offensive to Indians, must be restored. Strict limitations were imposed on the separation between Christians of different castes, as this had been practiced in the Jesuit mission from the beginning. Naturally the Jesuits, and others too, were incensed at the high-handed methods of Tournon, and at his total disregard for their views and ideas. Representations were made at Rome, and were successful in so far that a period of transition was permitted during which certain dispensations could be permitted. But in 1744 the Pope again took action to settle forever the question of the Malabar rites; no further dispensations could be permitted, and from now on the Christianity of India was to reflect in every detail the Christianity of Rome. Robert de Nobili's principle of "accommodation," the will to disrupt as little as possible the life and customs of the converts, was utterly rejected. Nearly two centuries were to pass before the official world of the Roman Catholic Church was again to take seriously the idea that Christianity need not necessarily be absolutely uniform in all the countries of the world.

All this was disagreeable and harmful to the pride and prestige of the Jesuits. But far worse was to follow. The Jesuits had become increasingly unpopular; their very success had made them an object of envy to other orders. They were accused of amassing enormous wealth through the commercial enterprises which they carried on for the support of their work, and of exercising harsh and authoritarian discipline on the Christians for whom they cared. In 1759 all Jesuits were ordered to leave Portuguese dominions. In 1773 the Order itself was dissolved by Pope Clement XIV in the Bull *Dominus ac Redemptor,* in which it was stated categorically that no future Pope might ever bring the Order back into existence. A small number of Jesuits transferred to other orders. A few lived on quietly in retirement in India. But the vast majority had to leave and to abandon the work to which they had dedicated their lives. The disaster was almost complete.

At this time two weaknesses in the Jesuit method of working came clearly into view.

In the first place, they had set before themselves extraordinarily high standards for the admission of Indian Christians to the priesthood and to the Society of Jesus itself. They had been at work in South India for well over two hundred years, yet they had put forward hardly a single Indian candidate for the priesthood. For this policy they could give good reason. In Goa the opposite policy had prevailed; the College of St. Paul had been turning out a steady stream of students, whom the bishops had ordained in large numbers; but in many cases these priests had brought discredit on their name by the looseness of their morals and their lack of zeal. The requirement that a priest must be celibate has always caused difficulties in a country where celibacy is unknown and is regarded as unnatural. The Jesuits had carried on their work largely through lay catechists, some of whom were without doubt men of great devotion and integrity. But a catechist cannot do precisely those things which from the Roman Catholic point of view are all-important: the celebration of Mass, the hearing of confessions, and the administration of extreme unction to the dying. After the expulsion of the Jesuits, attempts were made to replace them from other sources. The *Société des Missions Étrangères* sent in such priests as they could spare, but the number was wholly inadequate to meet the need. Goanese priests were sent in to take over the work on the Fisher Coast; but this substitution was hardly a success. Even Roman Catholic sources suggest that these priests took to themselves more than the authority of the foreign Jesuit, lived like princes, openly kept harems, and did little to honor the name of Christ or to maintain the reputation of the priesthood.

In the second place, the Jesuits had done hardly anything in the direction of the translation of the Holy Scriptures. In the early days of the missions in the sixteenth century, Roman Catholic authorities had taken a liberal view of the use of the Scriptures, regarding the translation of at least the New Testament into the local languages as one of the first duties of a missionary. The Council of Trent had taken a very different view; the use of the Scriptures was to be permitted to the laity only under the strictest safeguards, since an injudicious use of the Bible was known to produce and encourage heresy. Roman Catholic literature on a small scale had been developed in several Indian languages, and printing presses had been set up in a number of places. But it seems that the translation of the New Testament had not been completed in any of these tongues, and it is doubtful whether any part of it had ever been printed.

The concluding picture is sad. Great devotion had been manifested and great results had been achieved. Now, through a combination of political and ecclesiastical misfortunes it seemed that almost nothing was to be left. It has been reckoned that in the year 1750 there were roughly a million Christians in India, about one half in Goa and the other Portuguese possessions, a quarter in Kerala, the home of the Thomas Christians, and the remainder scattered throughout the rest of the country. It seems probable that by the end of the century this number had been reduced by half. Christianity had not died out, but it had been gravely weakened; the existing churches lacked zeal, courage and the hope of further great achievement. One chapter had ended; it was not clear what would be written in the next chapter, or whence the resources for a new beginning would be found.

III

PROTESTANTS EMERGE

A CHANGED SITUATION

WE HAVE SO FAR DEALT EXCLUSIVELY WITH ROMAN CATHOLIC missions. It is natural to ask the question, "Where were the Protestants in all this?" The answer is that they were hardly anywhere at all. In the first 150 years after the outbreak of the Reformation, the Protestant churches were so much occupied with the working out of their own positions, with their defense against the forces of the Counter-reformation, and with the solution of their own inner tensions, that they had little time or strength to consider a wider world and its claims upon them. Moreover, the nations of northern Europe came late to the task of discovery which had been so splendidly tackled by the Spaniards and the Portuguese, and in the sixteenth century were only beginning to think in imperial terms.

During the fifteenth century, in a series of remarkable edicts, successive Popes had divided the world between the kings of Spain and Portugal, had legitimized their rule over any lands newly discovered or yet to be discovered, and had given them extensive powers to act on behalf of the extension of Christ's kingdom in these lands. The Popes may well

48

have thought that they were determining the pattern for a thousand years. But the course of history set itself in a very different direction. The center of gravity moved steadily northwards and westwards; Spain and Portugal sank to the rank of second-class powers, and France, Britain and Holland, and later Germany and Norway, emerged as the great maritime nations of the earth. The history of the church is not the same as the history of the nations of the world; but it is an illusion to suppose that the church can exist within a vacuum; it is at every point influenced and in a measure conditioned by the events which are passing in the world around it. The Protestants rallied their forces very slowly, and their great missionary expansion did not take place till the nineteenth century; but as the sixteenth century passed over into the seventeenth, signs of the great change were already beginning to be apparent.

The first notable event was the formation of the British East India Company in 1600, to be followed two years later by the Dutch Company. British and Dutch, and then Danes, were determined to have their share in the vast new trade of the Asian lands; they took no account of the monopoly decreed by the Pope in favor of the Portuguese, and carried with them into Asia much of the rancor by which relations between Protestants and Roman Catholics were marked in Europe, especially in the period between 1618 and 1648, the lamentable era of the wars of religion.

The Dutch were more militant than the British. The capture of Cochin, Colombo, and later Macassar by their forces altered the entire balance of the world powers. The British came in peacefully, desiring nothing more than opportunities to trade. Their first settlement was at Surat on the west coast. To this they added Fort St. George (Madras) with an area of four square miles, purchased from the local ruler, and Fort St. David (Cuddalore). In 1690 Job Charnock founded Calcutta on a mud-flat in Bengal, and provided India with what was later to be its capital. When Charles II of England married a Portuguese princess, he was given the island of Bombay as a wedding-present, the Portuguese having failed to note that Bombay was potentially one of the great harbors of the world, and Charles being so little aware of its value that he leased it to the Company at a rent of £10 a year. By degrees a considerable number of Indians gathered themselves around the European settlements for purposes of trade and in order to enjoy the greater tranquility which was guaranteed by European stability and order. But there was no intention at that time on the part of the Western traders to carve out for themselves a dominion, and little interest in the evangelization of the local peoples.

ANGLICAN CHAPLAINS AND CONVERTS

The seventeenth century was, however, a pious age, and the English Company was far from careless about the spiritual welfare of those whom it sent out to distant places. Rules for the "factories" were strict, and included the injunction that prayers were to be said twice a day, as well as on Sundays. Whenever possible ships sailing for the East were provided with chaplains, and chaplains were appointed to all the main stations of the Company in India. When the first British ambassador to the court of the Great Mogul, Sir Thomas Roe, a pious man and later a notable ecumenist, arrived in India, he was accompanied by his chaplain. On the death of the first holder of this office, he wrote urgently for a replacement, and was sent the Reverend Edward Terry, Fellow of Clare College, Cambridge, to whose pen we owe a revealing book on the state of India at that time.

The supply of chaplains was always inadequate, and not all members of the class were edifying in their life and conduct. They were strictly forbidden to engage in the trading operations of the Company; but their salaries were small, and the majority of them seem to have yielded to the temptation to enrich themselves by taking part in everything that was going on. One chaplain was so successful in the pursuit of gain that on his return to England he was able to secure appointment to the bishopric of Bangor in Wales (1702), which he afterwards (1716) exchanged for the even more lucrative see of Meath, the premier bishopric of the Church of Ireland.[1]

Though the general standard may not have been high, a number of the chaplains earned a high reputation for godliness and devotion to their work. On the terrible night of the Black Hole of Calcutta (1756), one of those incarcerated was the Reverend Gervas Bellamy, a man greatly respected and beloved. When the night was over, he was found among the dead together with his favorite son John: "They were lying now, propped against the back wall, as though peacefully asleep. Gervas had a little smile on his face. John was wedged close beside him, as though determined to stay near his father to the end. Each was holding the other's hand."[2]

The main task of the chaplains was the spiritual care of Europeans, and of those of mixed race. The thought of conversion was not entirely absent, but the Company felt a responsibility not so much towards India as a whole as towards those Indians who were in the Company's service or dependent on its protection. Repeated references to this topic are found in the documents of the time. For instance, in 1698 strict injunctions were issued that chaplains were to learn Portuguese, the local *lingua franca*, in order that they might better instruct the "Gentoos" in the Christian faith. But in point of fact, only one baptism of an Indian by the Church of England is recorded in the seventeenth century. A Bengali boy had been brought to England in 1614 by one of the chaplains; the Company decided to educate him, so that "he might on occasion be sent unto his country, where God may be so pleased to make him an instrument in converting some of his nation." The boy was duly baptized in 1616 with the name Peter, but it does not appear that this promising beginning was ever followed up.[3]

---

1 This was the Reverend John Evans, in India from 1678 till 1690, when he was dismissed for being too actively engaged in trade. See F. Penny, *The Church in Madras*, pp. 665-666.

2 Noel Barber, *The Black Hole of Calcutta,* p. 225.

3 R. D. Paul, in his recent book *Triumphs of His Grace* has gathered together all that is known about Peter and his relations with the Rev-

THE DUTCH IN INDIA

The Dutch and the British were in agreement with one another in detesting Roman Catholics; they were almost as much in agreement in disliking one another. The struggle between them was long and keen; the final result was that the Dutch concentrated their efforts both in trade and in government on what is now called Indonesia, from which the British almost completely withdrew, whereas the British were left unhindered to develop the Indian market. The Dutch had a few strong settlements, as at Tuticorin and Negapatam in the south, and Chinsurah near Calcutta. Their influence, however, was local and restricted rather than general.

The Dutch also sent chaplains to India. From the areas previously occupied by the Portuguese all priests were expelled; the Dutch *predikants* took over the churches and congregations, and seem to have devoted themselves more to the subversion of Roman Catholics than to the evangelization of the heathen. Political and social advantages were held out to those who became Protestants, and by this means a large number were drawn over from their original faith. But success was not unqualified. It is recorded that when the distinguished preacher Philippus Baldaeus attempted to persuade some of the Parava Christians of the superiority of the Protestant faith, they replied to him, "Our great apostle Francis Xavier vindicated the truth of his Gospel by raising several people from the dead. If you will be good enough to follow his example, we shall be happy to pay attention to your words." In those regions Baldaeus did not make much progress.

We owe to the Dutch some excellent pieces of research into various aspects of Indian life. The great botanical work *Hortus Malabaricus,* which first appeared in 1678, was the work of a Dutch *predikant,* Johannes Caesarius. The above-mentioned Baldaeus produced a work on *The Superstitions of the Heathen in East India;* and his colleague Abraham Rogerius, who lived at Pulicat from 1631 to 1641, wrote a

---

erend Patrick Copland, who befriended him. "Peter: the first Indian Convert to Anglican Christianity," pp. 1-17.

book *Gentilismus Reseratus,* which two and a half centuries later was described by a highly competent authority as "still perhaps the most complete account of South Indian Hinduism, though by far the earliest."[4] Apart from these scholarly contributions, the Dutch exercised little influence beyond the limits of their own small settlements; at the end of the period of their activity Roman Catholicism was still the prevailing form of Christianity in India. For the first organized Protestant mission in India we have to wait until the dawn of the eighteenth century.

ENTER THE DANES

Like other northern nations, the Danes had been drawn into the Indian traffic, and had acquired one small property at Tranquebar not far from Pondicherry, and a second at Serampore near Calcutta. The pious chaplain of King Frederick IV, Franz Julius Lütkens, persuaded his royal master that he should follow the example of the Roman Catholic princes and set aside men and money to care for the spiritual welfare of his subjects in India. This was no call to the general evangelization of India. It was a deduction from the doctrine of the Christian prince, who is head of his subjects both in civil and in spiritual affairs and is answerable to God for their welfare. The king responded to the idea, and created the Danish Royal Mission. This was not to be an enterprise of the Church of Denmark. It was to be directed by a special corporation in Copenhagen created by the king; the missionaries were to be royal missionaries, appointed by the king and responsible to him.

No ministers were found in Denmark to undertake this new and difficult enterprise. Guided by Lütkens, the king turned to Halle, the great pietist center in Germany, and asked whether its director, August Hermann Francke, could find him candidates. Francke could and would. Two young men, Bartholomew Ziegenbalg and Henry Plütschau, were chosen and sent to Copenhagen, to be ordained there as a

---

[4] A. C. Burnell (1898), quoted in *Cambridge History of India,* vol. 5, p. 53.

further sign that, though the missionaries were German, this was a Danish mission. Things did not work out altogether smoothly. The bishop of Zealand examined the candidates and rejected them, perhaps disliking the pietistic type of theology in which Ziegenbalg had been trained at Halle. Some pressure appears to have been exercised from above, for the bishop relented and the ordination took place. On July 9, 1706, the first two Lutheran missionaries to India arrived at Tranquebar, a quiet and pleasant little town which still retains a good deal of its eighteenth century charm. No one wanted them; even the Danish chaplains were notably unfriendly. It is recorded that the two missionaries stood for hours in the burning heat, until some kind soul was willing to find them accommodation for the night.

Ziegenbalg was a tireless and copious letter-writer. His letters have been preserved in the archives at Halle, and not long ago were published by Professor Arno Lehmann under the title *Alte Briefe aus Indien*.[5] In these letters we are able to follow blow by blow the progress of the first Protestant mission in India. We learn what the missionaries wore, what they ate, and how they adapted themselves to the rigors of the climate. We read of the endless difficulties that they encountered, and of the beginnings of a missionary church.

The new missionaries had few precedents to work with. They were aware of the Roman Catholic missions in their neighborhood, but in many respects wished to dissociate themselves as completely as possible from them. At two points Ziegenbalg made decisions which were to be of lasting significance for all Protestant missions until the present time. First, it was decided that at the earliest possible date the New Testament must be translated and put into the hands of believers. Second, since believers must be able to read what is put into their hands, the school is an indispensable adjunct of the church. When a few years ago twenty-two coats of whitewash were stripped from an old building in the mission compound at Tranquebar, this was identified

---

5 A. Lehmann, *Alte Briefe aus Indien, 1706-1719*.

as the school which Ziegenbalg had founded within a year or two of the beginning of the mission.

The first task of Ziegenbalg was to learn the language, and this, as we have already had occasion to mention, was an exceedingly difficult task. Ziegenbalg never became such a profound scholar as Beschi, but it is clear that he set himself to master the high poetical style as well as the common speech of the people by whom he was surrounded. His mastery of the language was sufficient to enable him to produce a grammar which was of great service to later generations of missionaries. The language once learned, there was a further problem to be faced. There was no tradition of prose-writing in the Tamil language; almost the entire literature was in poetry, and of such an elaborate kind as to be unintelligible to ordinary people. It is true that Beschi had left behind a number of prose writings, some of them of excellent quality, but even here the poetic vocabulary had tended to creep in, and these writings were hardly on a level to be understood by simple people. For the Christian vocabulary, including such words as baptism, Ziegenbalg tended to take over the forms that had been developed by the Roman Catholics since the time of Robert de Nobili. This had the advantage of avoiding the creation of a second form of Christian utterance; the drawback was that few of these terms were related to the current speech of the people, most of them having been drawn from Sanskrit sources. Apart from this, Ziegenbalg decided that simplicity and intelligibility were to be the criteria for his work.

After seven years the first great work was completed; the New Testament lay ready, the first complete translation, as it appears today, into any Indian language. How was it to be printed? Here we encounter a pleasing example of early ecumenical cooperation. The husband of Queen Anne of England was a Danish prince; with him was his chaplain, the Lutheran Anton Wilhelm Böhme, through whom interest in the Danish Tranquebar mission entered England. On the one occasion on which Ziegenbalg returned to Europe, he was welcomed in London, lionized, and made the object of a great deal of public attention. It seemed only natural that Böhme should suggest to the high Anglican Society for Promoting Christian Knowledge that they should send a printing press to India for the service of the mission. Thus it came about that the Tamil New Testament, translated by a German in the service of the Danish crown, was printed on an English printing press.[6] Ziegenbalg before his death had made considerable progress with the translation of the Old Testament. He was well aware that his labors on so gigantic a task could only be rough and preparatory, and that many hands would have to join in the work before a satisfactory translation could emerge. Unfortunately his successors took far less pains than he; the work was too quickly done, and the results were far from satisfactory. Not until the end of the century, when another outstanding German missionary, Philip Fabricius, took the task in hand, was a complete translation of the Bible produced. This translation has served as the basis for all future revisions.

One further sign of the wisdom and foresight of this astonishing man, Ziegenbalg, was that he realized at an early date that what he had come to India to do was to bring into being an Indian and not a European church. Only three years after his arrival in Tranquebar, he was writing to Denmark that one of the members of the mission should be given the *potestas ordinandi,* the authority to ordain, in order that the church in India might not be dependent for its ministry upon a distant and Western church. However, steps for the creation of an Indian ministry were not taken during the life of Ziegenbalg. The first ordination of an Indian catechist, Aaron, to the full ministry of the church took place in 1733; but the seed had been well and truly sown by the founder of the mission.[7]

Ziegenbalg had realized from the start that if the gospel is to be preached in India, it cannot be preached in a

---

[6] The fount of Tamil type had, however, been cast in Halle. See H. W. Gensichen, " 'Abominable Heathenism'; A rediscovered tract by Bartolomaeus Ziegenbalg," *Indian Church History Review,* I, 1 (1967), 29ff.

[7] On Aaron, see R. D. Paul, *Chosen Vessels,* pp. 1-23.

vacuum; the missionary must be aware of the mind and outlook of those to whom he is to preach. For this reason, he
took the trouble to make a minute study of the habits and
customs, the beliefs and the ideas, of the people among whom
he lived, and in the end wrote down his discoveries in a book
with the title *The Genealogy of the Malabarian Gods*. He sent
the manuscript to Europe, with the request that it should
be printed; but European opinion at that time had not
yet caught up with the idea that ethnological and anthropo-
logical research is part of the missionary calling. Ziegenbalg
received the rather unkind answer that his task was to pro-
claim the eternal gospel in India and not to propagate
heathen superstition in Europe. The book lay in the archives
at Halle for 150 years, until it was discovered by the distinguished missionary scholar Wilhelm Germann, and published in both German and English.

Ziegenbalg died in 1719, after only thirteen years of service
and at the age of thirty-six. The more his work is studied, the
more astonishing it becomes that he was able to accomplish
so much under such immense difficulties, and in so short a
time.

EXTENSIONS OF THE MISSION

In the eighteenth century it was taken for granted that
one who went out as a missionary went for life; his new
country was to become his home. In point of fact, of the
fifty-six missionaries who served the Danish mission in the
eighteenth century, only fifteen returned to Europe. More
than one of them resided in Tranquebar for sixty years. The
church began to grow. A little intimate society of missionaries and Indian Christians grew up, retired from the world
and exercising little influence on the life of the rest of India.
Tranquebar was a tiny territory; within a comparatively few
years it had been thoroughly evangelized, and though the
majority of the people remained Hindus, there was little
scope for expansion or for adventurous outreach into the non-
Christian world. Naturally some among the younger missionaries found themselves drawn into areas beyond the limits of

the Danish colony, and encountered great new fields of opportunity. The British authorities were suspicious of foreigners, but having found the German missionaries upright and
inoffensive persons, they gave permission for residence and
for the opening of schools in the two main British centers
in South India, Madras and Cuddalore.

At once the mission was faced with a new problem. The
king of Denmark made it clear that he was providing funds
for Christian work within his own territories and nowhere
else; if the missionaries cared to go beyond the Danish territories, they might do so, but the king could accept no further responsibility for them. What was to be done? Once
again an ecumenical solution was found. The Society for
Promoting Christian Knowledge, already deeply committed
to an interest in the mission, came forward with funds and
a readiness to take into its service these German Lutherans
who had not received and would never receive ordination
according to the Anglican rite. Thus came into existence
what came to be known as the English mission, though no
Englishman ever entered its service and though the connection was rather financial and administrative than ecclesiastical. The German missionaries, however, showed their gratitude by such actions as the translation of the English Book
of Common Prayer into Tamil, and by a willingness to minister also to Europeans, especially to those in the service of
the Company. Thus a considerable number of the German
missionaries, Gericke and Fabricius in Madras, Pohle in
Trichinopoly, and others, spent the greater part of their
missionary lives in the service of an English and Anglican
missionary society.

The same was true of the greatest of all the missionaries
who served in India in this period, Christian Friedrich
Schwartz, who arrived in India in 1750, and served until his
death in 1798 without once returning to Europe.[8] Schwartz

---

[8] There is, unfortunately, no good modern life of Schwartz in English.
The *Memoirs* by Hugh Pearson, D.D., 2 vols. (London: J. Hatchard & Son,
1835), is a missionary classic, but the style will strike the contemporary
reader as ponderous.

was no genius. He was rather the supreme example of what steady Christian devotion, diligence, and self-discipline can make of a man. He must have had good natural gifts, as is evident from his having mastered Tamil and Portuguese, to which he later added Hindustani, Marathi, and Persian. But such of his sermons as have survived give evidence of earnestness rather than brilliance, and he left no writings of any notable caliber. Yet his character made an indelible impression on the minds of those who encountered him; all speak of his cheerfulness and humility, his ability to get along with all kinds of men, and his utter integrity and selflessness. It is remarkable that when he died, the same East India Company which was setting itself to chase all missionaries out of Bengal erected a memorial tablet in the Fort Church at Madras with a glowing tribute to the character and ministry of the alien preacher of the gospel.[9]

Schwartz spent the first twelve years of his service in Tranquebar, and there was nothing in this period to set him markedly apart from his colleagues. In 1762 he moved to Trichinopoly, and at once a wider field of service opened before him. Here there was a British garrison, and before long Schwartz was employed as chaplain both to the Europeans and to the Indian soldiers in the Company's regiments. Sixteen years later he moved again to Tanjore, the capital of a small Indian kingdom, and remained there till the end of his life. The fame of the "royal priest of Tanjore" grew until he was one of the best-known men in India.

The confidence evoked by Schwartz's integrity led him into a number of employments of a kind that are unusual for a missionary. When the Company's government wished to send an embassy to Haidar Ali, the Muslim tyrant of Mysore, Schwartz was persuaded to join the emissaries, a step entirely approved by Haidar Ali, who remarked, "Send me the Christian; he will not let me down." When Tanjore was threatened with siege by the Muslim forces, and the peasants were unwilling to yield up the grain indispensably necessary for the provisioning of the fort, it was only the promise of

9 Quoted in full in Pearson, *op. cit.*, vol. 2, pp. 411-413.

Schwartz that they would be paid in full that led them to withdraw their objections. The young heir to the throne of Tanjore, Serfojee, was placed under the care of Schwartz, who saw to his education. The prince never became a Christian; but one of the most touching tributes to Schwartz is a simple poem written in English by his protégé.[10] At one time the missionary served as Diwan, or prime minister of the kingdom; but, however pressed with public business, he would always find time to teach in the Christian school and to instruct candidates for baptism. Under his care, the Christian fellowship grew to a membership of 2,800.

Schwartz died a rich man, since for a considerable time he had been drawing a large salary and had received many gifts; but he left all to the mission, and is commemorated among other things by the high school in Ramnad which still bears his name. He left another legacy to posterity. In 1787 he ordained to the ministry his foster son, the younger Kohloff, son of one of the Tranquebar missionaries. Kohloff took over the work in Tanjore and served there for a period of more than fifty years. His son continued to serve in the Anglican mission, the three Kohloffs between them having contributed 150 years to the service of the church in India.

DECLINE AND NEW HOPES

The work of the Danish mission, with its English branch, was never on a large scale. It has been calculated that in the first century of its existence 34,970 persons had been baptized, of whom perhaps half were alive at the end of the eighteenth century. When the difficulties of pioneer work and the strength of the opposition are taken into account, this may seem no inconsiderable achievement. But towards the end of the century the mission sank into a gradual decline; missionary enthusiasm in Europe was at a low ebb with the growth of rationalistic views in the churches; replacements were not sent out, and new enterprises were hardly possible. The Protestant missions seemed to be af-

[10] Pearson, *op. cit.*, vol. 2, p. 397. Serfojee Rajah died in 1834.

flicted by the same diseases that had brought the Roman Catholic Church in India into a state of dire weakness.

And yet, at the last moment, a strange and unaccountable event took place. Schwartz had extended his journeys to the district of Tirunelveli in the extreme south, and to its capital Palamcottah. Here he had found, or had founded, a small congregation. Then, just at the end of the century, in circumstances that have never been fully explained, a great movement broke out not far from Cape Comorin, the southernmost point of India. Those affected were the Shanars (Nadars), a hardy people who made their living by climbing the palmyra tree to draw from it the sweet juice which is the local substitute for sugar. The Nadars, a rough and vigorous people, who have shown a remarkable capacity for development under the influence of education, were not untouchable, but had no access to Hindu temples. It was perhaps their ambiguous status that made them so readily accessible to the Christian gospel. Between May 30, 1800, and June 24, 1803, the Lutheran missionaries baptized 5,670 of these people. It is not clear what amount of preparation had been given them, or what provision was made for their care afterwards. The whole district was left in the charge of Satyanathan, one of the most faithful and gifted of the Indian pastors. In this remote and obscure corner of the world the foundations of a living church had been laid.[11]

---

[11] Full details are given by Bishop R. Caldwell in *The Early History of the Tinnevelly Mission*, pp. 70-78. Caldwell carefully discusses the motives of the converts, and comes down firmly on the side of their sincerity. When he published his book, he had been working for forty years in the same area.

IV

FREE FOR ALL

A CHANGED POLITICAL SITUATION

THE POLITICAL SITUATION IN INDIA AT THE END OF THE EIGHT-
eenth century was almost as different as could be imagined
from that which had prevailed at the beginning of the
century.

The eighteenth century was not far advanced before it
became plain that the Mogul dominion was breaking up. The
emperor was still there in Delhi and nominally ruled; but
his control was becoming feebler, the provinces were assert-
ing an ever-increasing independence, and it seemed inevitable
that India should break up again into a congeries of small
kingdoms, ravaged by internecine and endemic war. Was it
possible that one other single power would emerge, capable
of holding India together in unity, and keeping peace between its many regions?

As we have seen, it was not part of the policy of the
European nations to conquer large areas of India. But now
the imperial dream was born in the brain of a single man.
The brilliant governor of the French settlement at Pondicherry, Joseph François Dupleix, saw the new possibilities

in the situation.[1] The strategy should be to make alliances
with some of the local rulers, to set the Indian states at one
another's throats, to maintain a small professional army
but to train a much larger number of Indians to fight under
the direction of French officers. If this policy were followed,
it should be possible within a comparatively few years to
make France the dominant power in India and the heir of
the Mogul empire. With a little more understanding of his
projects in France itself, and a little more luck in the field,
Dupleix might have achieved his aims. As events turned out,
however, where he had shown the way another entered in
and reaped the harvest. Through a series of victories culminating in the battle of Plassey on June 23, 1757, Robert Clive
shattered the dreams of the French and made it clear that
in the future Britain would be the strongest power in India.

Nothing could have been further from the intentions of
the heads of the East India Company; they were in India to
trade and for no other purpose. Then, and at many later
times, they signified their disapproval, and did their utmost
to prevent any further acquisition of territory. But there
seems to be a fatal momentum in colonial expansion. Once
a colonial power has begun to take over the lands of weaker
peoples, it seems impelled by an irresistible law to continue
expanding until the natural frontiers are reached, or until
it clashes with the ambitions of another power advancing in
the opposite direction. British dominion in India was acquired by many and devious ways. In South India the British
appeared not as conquerors but as deliverers from the menace
of the Muslim warriors of Mysore; hence the much better relations between the British and the Indians in South India
than elsewhere. Sometimes, as in Sind, advance took place
through sheer aggression. The Punjab was taken over as
the result of a successful war against a power which, if un-
subdued, would have been strong enough to constitute a
permanent threat to British rule. The end was in sight.

---

1 There is a life of Dupleix in English: Colonel Malleson, C.S.I., *Dupleix* in the *Rulers of India* series. Dupleix was governor of Pondicherry
from 1741 to 1754.

Though a third of the territory and a quarter of the population of the subcontinent were left under the direct rule of Indian princes, in fact the word of the colonial power was the only word that carried weight. For the first time in history the entire subcontinent from Cape Comorin to the Khyber Pass was a single political unit. Peace reigned instead of war, and the ordinary man gradually began to enjoy tranquility such as he had never previously known.

It might have been thought that the advent of a nominally Christian power would have been favorable to the spread of Christian missions. The contrary was the case. The British rulers were convinced that their rule was precarious and unpopular, as at first it certainly was. It was their aim to disturb their subjects as little as possible and to maintain the ancient ways. This policy was carried so far that British administrators found themselves responsible for the financial affairs of Hindu temples and for the organization of Hindu festivals, acting, as was caustically said in England, as "church-warden of Juggernaut and dry-nurse of Vishnu." To such a government the presence of missionaries could not but be unwelcome. Roman Catholics were automatically under suspicion as foreigners. British missionaries would be likely to insult the religious feelings of the natives, and, still worse, through education to instil into their minds Western ideas of liberty which would consort ill with the ideas of government which the Company entertained. In consequence the new rulers made up their minds to exclude all missionaries from their territories. This policy was carried so far that two young missionaries who had managed to enter Bengal without permits were arrested, put on board a ship, and compelled to work their passage back to Europe as common sailors before the mast.

On the whole, English society, in so far as it knew anything about the situation, was inclined to agree with this policy. But the great evangelical movements of the eighteenth century had brought into being a considerable body of Christians who were missionary-minded and adopted a very different point of view. Every twenty years the Charter of the Company had to be renewed by the British Parliament; might this not be the moment at which action could be taken to open India to the presence of missionaries? The first attempt was made in 1793. This was mainly the work of Charles Grant, who as a young civil servant in India had undergone a deep experience of conversion, and for forty years until his death in 1823, both in Calcutta and later in London, exercised an immense influence on Indian affairs. It was Charles Grant who put forward the so-called pious clause, which contained the remarkable words that "the . . . Court of Directors . . . are hereby empowered and required to send out, from time to time . . . fit and proper persons as schoolmasters, missionaries or otherwise . . . and to provide for the necessary and decent maintenance of the persons to be so sent out." The clause was thrown out. At the time this seemed to be a defeat for the evangelical forces; in a longer perspective we can see that this was the best thing that could have happened. It would have been a fatal handicap if the missions had come in under the patronage of the alien government, and in close financial dependence upon it.

In 1813 the Christian forces tried again. A great debate was held, in which one of the old guard earnestly invited Parliament to consider "what will have been gained to ourselves by giving them Calvinism and fermented liquors; and whether predestination and gin would be a compensation to the natives of India for the changes which will overwhelm their habits, morals and religion."[2] But opinion had considerably changed in twenty years. The Evangelicals did not obtain as much as they had hoped, but two substantial gains could be recorded. The government agreed to the establishment of an Anglican bishopric of Calcutta; and permission for the residence of Europeans in India was granted in terms which clearly included missionaries. The long campaign did not really end until 1833; in the charter of that year, all restrictions were removed, and it was possible for missionaries of all races and all Christian confessions to enter and

---

[2] For this debate and its consequences, see J. C. Marshman, *The Life and Times of Carey, Marshman, and Ward,* vol. 2, pp. 1-51.

to settle wherever they would in British India, and in Indian states whose rulers did not object to their presence.

During this same period it is possible to mark the beginnings of that sense of imperial responsibility which in course of time was to make of British rule in India a trusteeship, directed consciously to the well-being of all the inhabitants. The question of how much a foreign ruler may interfere in the habits and customs of his subjects is a delicate one. At one point the governor-general of the time, Lord William Bentinck, decided that intervention was necessary; henceforth the custom of the burning of Hindu widows on their husbands' pyres, the so-called *Satī*, must cease. This was a courageous decision. Bentinck was warned that the agitation which was certain to result might threaten British rule in India. But once his mind was made up, Bentinck did not hesitate. On December 4, 1829, *Satī* was irrevocably forbidden. After brief agitation the Hindu world settled down to the new order, and, as we are told by one who knew the situation first hand, in twenty years' time the Indians, jealous of their national honor, were prepared to affirm that the custom had never existed.[3]

This was the first of a series of notable enactments which gradually brought undesirable practices under control, and by cautious steps freed the Indian Christian from some of the disabilities under which he had long suffered.

ENGLAND AWAKES

The year 1793 was notable not only for the rejection of the "pious clause." In June of that same year the former cobbler and Baptist preacher William Carey set out with his family for India. England was now to enter in person into the field in which the British churches had so long been indirectly interested.

The beginnings of Carey's Indian career were inauspicious. He had no permit to reside in India. For five years the only way in which he could escape arrest and find means to maintain his family was to take service as manager of an indigo

---

[3] Marshman, *op. cit.*, vol. 2, p. 417.

plantation in the interior of Bengal. Here little missionary work was possible; but Carey was able to lay the foundations for his splendid knowledge of the Bengali language. In 1800 the situation changed completely with the arrival of two colleagues, Joshua Marshman, a charity schoolmaster, and William Ward, a printer. The new arrivals fell upon the excellent idea of setting up the mission at the little Danish settlement of Serampore, only sixteen miles from Calcutta, where, though watched by the jealous eyes of the English Company, they would be safe under the Danish flag from any hostile measures. Thus came into being the famous partnership which was to last unbroken for almost thirty years.

Carey and his colleagues had clear ideas as to the lines which missionary endeavor should follow. The first step must be the translation, printing and dissemination of the Scriptures in all the main languages of the East. Carey himself performed the astonishing feat of translating the entire Bible into Bengali, Sanskrit and Marathi. In a little over thirty years parts of the Scriptures had been printed in no less than thirty-seven languages, including Chinese. All these versions were rough and stood in need of revision. It might have been better if the Serampore trio had cast their net less widely, and had concentrated more on excellence than on extension. They were self-taught men who lacked the finer points of scholarship. Moreover, their knowledge of many of the languages with which they dealt was still in a rudimentary stage. Nevertheless, the achievement stands unequaled in the whole history of Christian missionary work.

In the second place, the Serampore trio believed in the widest possible dissemination of Christian knowledge by means of preaching. But if this was to be effective, the preacher must be armed with good knowledge of the manners and customs of his hearers. To this end the missionaries devoted themselves to a careful study of Hinduism, and to the translation of some of the Hindu classics — in the opinion of their friends in England, this time might have been better devoted to other things.

Thirdly, the Serampore trio believed that as soon as converts came in, they should be organized into churches which from the start would give them responsibilities as being the body of Christ. One of the first acts of the missionaries, when the community had been brought into order in Serampore, was to organize a church with William Ward as the pastor. As missionaries the trio were subject to the orders of the Baptist Missionary Society in England, but their church was their own. The Baptist system of independent local churches lent itself well to this beginning of a genuinely Indian church in India.

Carey and his friends maintained the warmest possible relationships with Christians of other denominations. They were, therefore, prepared in 1806 to accept enthusiastically an unexpected fellow worker in the person of Henry Martyn, one of the new race of "pious" chaplains sent out from England under the influence of Charles Simeon. Unlike his Baptist friends, Martyn had received the best education which the day afforded and had a wholly exceptional gift for languages. This led at times to minor strains. The Cambridge scholar could not refrain from criticizing the imperfections of the versions put out by the pioneers; they in their turn found it hard to be criticized by one so much younger, who had in a sense climbed in on the top of their great achievements. Yet mutual relationships of affection and esteem were never for long disturbed.[4] Martyn's own contribution was unique. In his brief years of service in India he completed a version of the New Testament in Urdu, which after many revisions is still the basis of the version which is in use today. He had carried through a thorough revision of the Persian, and he was deeply involved in the Arabic. In 1813, at the age of thirty-one, he died alone at Tokat in Asiatic Turkey, in a desperate attempt to return to England and there to recover his health.

We have yet to mention one of the most remarkable of

---

[4] Carey wrote of Martyn, "as the image or shadow of bigotry is not known among us here, we take sweet counsel together, and go to the house of God as friends." Marshman, *op. cit.*, vol. 1, p. 246.

all the enterprises of Serampore. Carey had seen at an early date that the evangelization of India could not be carried out by a handful of missionaries; it must be the aim of the missionary to send out much larger numbers of competent and well-trained Indian witnesses into the field. For the simpler people village catechists would do. But the Indian church would soon need an intellectual elite, equal to the missionaries in knowledge and able to meet learned non-Christians on their own level. So was born the splendid idea of a "College for the instruction of Asiatic, Christian and other youth, in Eastern Literature and European Science." The college came into existence in 1819. The king of Denmark became interested and gave to the college, which was still in Danish territory, the right to award the degrees of Bachelor of Arts and Bachelor of Divinity.

The splendid idea was premature. Students were few, and it was difficult to recruit teachers of a caliber adequate to maintain the great fabric. Later generations allowed the college to become something very different from what had been intended by the founders. Yet all was not lost. Just about a century after the original foundation, Serampore was reorganized as a center for graduate theological training, awarding to its students the degree of Bachelor of Divinity, and serving as a central point of organization for theological training in almost all the non-Roman churches in India.

BEGINNINGS IN THE SOUTH

The Christians baptized during the remarkable mass movement in the Tirunelveli district had long been left isolated under the care of Indian pastors. Ignorance was profound, but the great majority of them had stood firm and had not reverted to Hinduism. A new day dawned when in 1816 a "pious" chaplain, the Rev. James Hough, later historian of the Church in India,[5] was appointed to Palamcottah. Although it was no direct responsibility of his, Hough inter-

---

[5] Hough's five volumes appeared between 1839 and 1850. He is copious and reliable, but his work is marred by a fanatical dislike of the Roman Catholic Church.

ested himself in the Indian Christians, secured for them copies of the Bible and the Prayer Book in Tamil, and encouraged the pastors in their work. When in 1820 the time came for him to leave, he invited the Church Missionary Society to come in and build on the foundation that had twice been laid. The Society sent Charles Theophilus Ewald Rhenius, a German who had come into the service of the Anglican society by way of the missionary training center in Berlin.

No better choice could have been made. Rhenius was a missionary of some years' experience, with an excellent knowledge of the Tamil language, which he put to good use in the composition of a grammar that is still serviceable. He proved himself a splendid organizer. The basis of the mission was to be the village school, the teacher of which was also to be the village catechist. Many of these were men of little education, but under careful supervision they grew in knowledge and Christian character, and in time became the pillars of a great Christian movement. Later missionaries did little to improve on the system worked out by Rhenius. To him we owe the practice that in 700 villages in the Tirunelveli diocese the bell rings every evening to call the Christians together for Evensong.

From village after village came an appeal for teaching and for help. At the time of the death of Rhenius in 1838 there were Christian groups in nearly three hundred villages over an area of about 2,000 square miles. For the first time an organized village church was coming into being in India. Unhappily the last years of Rhenius were darkened by a deep disagreement with the Church Missionary Society. In 1835 the Society insisted that, since a bishop was now available in India, ordinations in the future should be episcopal; Rhenius wished to retain the older Tranquebar system, under which the missionaries had themselves ordained catechists to the ministry as the need arose. Rhenius left the service of the Church Missionary Society, but unfortunately remained in Palamcottah and split in two the church which he had so successfully guided. After his death in 1838, harmony was gradually restored, the dark period was forgotten, and the Tirunelveli Church was glad to recognize in Rhenius its third founder, after Schwartz and Hough.

Shortly before the arrival in South India of James Hough, a servant of the London Missionary Society, W. T. Ringeltaube, was invited by a convert from the depressed classes to settle in the village of Mayiladi in South Travancore, not far from the borders of Tirunelveli. Here his work prospered so much that between 1806 and 1815 he was able to baptize about a thousand persons. These belonged to various castes, but the majority were from among the Shanars, the same people that had responded so well on the other side of the border. Ringeltaube, a lonely man who often suffered from bouts of depression, wondered at times whether there had been any deep and genuine response to the gospel. Perhaps he had expected too much of new converts from a deeply pagan background, but he need not have been anxious. When Ringeltaube himself disappeared in 1815, in circumstances that have never been cleared up, the work passed into the hands of able successors, spread and grew, until the movement equaled in strength that directed by their Anglican colleagues in Tirunelveli.

It was in South India that a great missionary controversy was fought out, to the lasting benefit of the Indian church. The Tranquebar missionaries had from time to time ordained experienced catechists, though never more than one at a time. The idea had grown up in British missionary circles that the Indian clergyman ought to have the same kind of training and possess the same kind of knowledge as his missionary colleagues. As a result, in 1842 there were in the Tirunelveli area eighteen ordained missionaries, and one ordained Indian, the Reverend John Devasahayam. It was clear, with the church growing rapidly, that if the ministry of the church was to be a ministry of the Word *and sacraments,* some radical changes would have to be made. The challenge came from an exceptionally able Welshman, John Thomas, who in his remote station of Megnanapuram, "the village of true wisdom," was performing marvels in turning a physical and spiritual wilderness into the garden of the Lord. He maintained, against all opposition, that the right course would be to take the best of the village catechists, train them in their own language in the elements of theology, and ordain them to the full ministry of the church. In the end Thomas had his way. The first ordination class of six men met for three years in the tower room of what was later the Cathedral of Palamcottah, and all members of the group were ordained in 1851. The experiment proved such a success that it was never again called into question; the same method was followed in many areas, with the understanding that the time would come in which the Indian church would need and would produce ministers of a higher educational standard.

SCOTLAND TAKES A HAND

The Church of Scotland entered only slowly and hesitantly into the missionary arena. When it did so, it opened up a new epoch of missionary work.

The main successes of the missions in India had been won in the villages and among uneducated people. Alexander Duff, who arrived from Edinburgh in 1830, was convinced that the time had come in which the Christian challenge must be presented to the elite of India. The method by which this could be achieved was education in the English language, but on a firmly Christian basis. Duff had arrived at the appropriate moment. There was a stirring of intellectual interest among the young people in Calcutta, and an openness to new ideas such as had been almost wholly lacking in the eighteenth century. Here was the chance, and Duff was ready to seize it. Within a few months he had opened what later became the General Assembly's Institution. On July 13, 1830, he stood before the first class, and as the first act of the day read out slowly and solemnly the Lord's Prayer in Bengali, and then invited some of the boys themselves to read from the Christian Scriptures. Before long Duff had around him 200 intelligent boys of the highest castes, who were beginning to make rapid progress in the English language.

The first tangible results came after two years, when between August 1832 and April 1833 four young men of high caste accepted Jesus Christ and confessed their faith in him through baptism. Nothing like this had been known since the days of Robert de Nobili in Madura. The furore was immense, and for a time the whole work was threatened. But such was the excellence of Duff's school that society could not do without it, and before long the place was again full of eager schoolboys. The number of conversions was not large: thirty-six in all the years that Duff served in India. But almost all were men of distinction, who laid the foundation for some of the great Christian families of India, and rendered outstanding service in the ministry of the Christian church. Beyond the circle of those who were baptized the Christian message and its influence spread into countless families of the well-to-do.

Duff was not alone in his efforts. Two years later he was followed by John Wilson, who founded in Bombay the college that was later to win lasting fame as Wilson College. Wilson was a greater scholar than Duff and acquired a deeper knowledge of India and its languages. Extremely interesting were his contacts with the Parsis, the Zoroastrian refugees who made Bombay their home and flourished in wealth and in the exercise of good works. The Parsis were so sure that no Parsi boy could ever be converted that they readily sent their sons to school. When the son of one of the leading Parsi families was converted, their fury and amazement knew no bounds.

Wilson was followed by the Anglican Robert Noble, who in Masulipatam in the Telugu area brought into being in 1843 the school (later college) which was subsequently called by his name. Two years later Stephen Hislop founded a college in Nagpur in the very heart of India. In Tirunelveli the blind Anglo-Indian Cruikshank expounded the Scriptures to young Hindus with such effect that a number of them came forward to be baptized.[6]

---

[6] I have just been reading old letters of 1847, in which the name of the first convert, Tiruvengidam, repeatedly occurs. This young man, who

In 1837 Anderson and Braithwaite founded in the city of Madras the Institution, the parent of what is now called the Madras Christian College, in some ways the most distinguished Christian institution in India, which under a succession of notable principals has trained a Christian elite for India, and brought thousands of students of higher caste into contact with the teachings of the gospel.

In almost every case, the course of events was the same. After a somewhat prolonged introductory period, a small group of students would become interested in what they had heard. Out of this group a yet smaller group would make up its mind to follow Christ in baptism. As soon as this became known, the school or college would be almost empty, the parents having withdrawn their sons in panic. On a number of occasions the missionaries were brought into court on charges of abduction or of undue influence on their charges. Fortunately all of these teachers had been very cautious as to the manner in which they exercised their ministry. They had refrained from baptizing minors, and had no difficulty in showing that those who had become Christians had done so out of free choice and in the light of their own honest convictions. In every case they were exonerated. Some converts disappeared and were never seen again, smuggled away to distant places by their relatives, or hurried out of this world. Almost all the others had to leave their families with no hope of ever returning — such was the strictness with which the rule of caste was observed. There was no course open to the missionaries other than that of taking the young men into their homes, treating them as their own sons, and caring for them until they could find their own way in the world and support themselves by the exercise of some profession. This was undesirable; it led to the Westernization of the converts to a degree that the missionaries would gladly have avoided, and reduced them to a state of dependence on their Western friends that made difficult the development of in-

---

took the name William Thomas Sattianadhen, became the founder of a regular Christian dynasty; his great-great-grandson is today a leading presbyter of the Church of South India.

dependent character and action. Happily the results in a great many cases were far better than might have been expected.

In the course of nearly a century and a half the Christian colleges of India have changed in character, and to some extent in purpose. But the church has never gone back from the way opened up by Alexander Duff. There were in 1968 no less than 130 Christian colleges of university standard with a total of 117,000 students, nearly one-tenth of all university students in India, though Christians make up less than 3 per cent of the population. All of Duff's early students were non-Christians; today 39 per cent of the students are Christians. In the days of Carey and Duff, even the most progressive missionaries hardly thought of the education of women up to university level; today more than forty Christian colleges in India are for women only, this being a field in which, as in the education of boys, the missionaries were the pioneers.

MISSIONARY PENETRATION

The first half of the nineteenth century was the period in which the number of missionary societies in India very rapidly increased, as a result on the one hand of the growing sense of responsibility of the Western churches, and on the other as a result of the new freedom of access which was guaranteed by the successive revisions of the charter of the East India Company. Specially notable was the arrival of large numbers of missionaries from the United States of America and from the continent of Europe.

First of the American societies to arrive was the American Board of Commissioners for Foreign Missions, who were successful in setting up a small cause in Bombay in 1813. Greater success was to attend their work in South India. In 1835 John Scudder, who had arrived in Ceylon in 1819, moved to Madura, the scene of the labors of Robert de Nobili, and set up one of the first medical missions in India. In 1853 two of his sons moved to Arcot and developed a work which later was to pass under the control of the American Dutch

Reformed Church, and continues to the present day. The Scudders developed a dynasty of missionaries, comparable only to that of the Kohloffs, which continued from generation to generation over more than a century.

American Presbyterians of various sections of that large community found their field in the Punjab and a little later in the United Provinces, now Uttar Pradesh. Among their most distinguished members was Charles W. Forman, who arrived in 1848, spent more than forty years in India, and was instrumental in founding in Lahore a college which is still known by his name.

Anglicans had begun to dig themselves more deeply into the soil of India. The original bishopric, as we have seen, was founded in 1813. The first bishop, Thomas F. Middleton, had great ideas for the development of an Indian ministry, and founded Bishop's College, Calcutta, an institution which like Serampore proved to be premature, since the summit of a pyramid cannot firmly exist unless the base of the pyramid is wide enough to support it. A century later, however, it took on new life as the premier Anglican college for theological education. The second bishop, Reginald Heber, author of a number of the best hymns in the English language, made a deeper impression on Christian society in India than perhaps any other churchman in so short a time, but he survived only three years, too short a time to leave any memorable contribution to the Christian enterprise. In 1835 the Anglican episcopate was enlarged by the formation of the bishoprics of Madras and Bombay. The first bishop of Madras, Daniel Corrie, had been one of the "pious" chaplains and a friend and associate of Henry Martyn.

The Anglican Church Missionary Society, working mainly with German missionaries, notable among them John James Weitbrecht, had won one considerable success in Bengal; in the Nadiya district in a time of famine a large number of Hindus put themselves under instruction and eventually received baptism. This was thought by many to be the dawn of a new day of Christian victory. But in fact the movement never grew far beyond the original achievement, perhaps because the missionaries did too much for the converts and failed to develop in them the spirit of independence and self-help. The Nadiya Church became the typical example of an encapsulated Christian community, continuing to exist but showing no power to extend itself within the Hindu community which surrounded it.

The great achievement of the Church Missionary Society was in extending itself right across North India, in that Ganges plain which was the original home of Hinduism, and in which Hinduism existed in its classical and least approachable form. Amritsar, the home of the Golden Temple of the Sikhs, was reached in 1852, and Peshawar on the northwest frontier, in an almost exclusively Muslim area, in 1855. In a number of cases the stations of the Church Missionary Society were founded in response to requests from Christian members of the Indian Civil Service, and in part at least subsidized by these Christian laymen, who unofficially regarded the propagation of the Christian faith as part of their responsible service in India.[7]

The continental forces, so long represented by the Danish Mission alone, began to recover strength towards the middle of the century, and to enter into various parts of India.

The Basel Mission, which had contributed some of the most distinguished missionaries of the Church Missionary Society, in 1834 began its own work in South Canara in southwest India. One of the outstanding contributions of the Basel Mission was in the field of industrial mission. Believing that Christian converts should be able to support themselves, the mission developed in Mangalore two notable industries: textiles and the manufacture of tiles. Basel Mission tiles were for many years a synonym for excellence; this work was carried on till the outbreak of the first world war in 1914. The most remarkable member of this mission was Samuel

---

[7] One of the most outstanding of these Christian rulers was James Thomason, son of one of the "pious" chaplains, who was lieutenant-governor of the northwestern provinces from 1844 to 1853. The records of his life make it plain that he most scrupulously observed religious neutrality in every action of his official life.

Hebich, a pietist with revivalistic tendencies, whose most successful work was carried out not among Hindus, but among the British officers of the garrison at Cannanore. Hebich's methods were unconventional in the extreme, but his success was so great that at one time one of the British regiments was known by the unofficial title of "Hebich's Own," an honorific title generally reserved for the members of the British royal family. At a somewhat later date the work of Hebich came in for bitter criticism from a Swiss pastor, Ernst Friedrich Langhans, who gave to one chapter of his critical survey the rather uncomplimentary title, "Results and Humbug." A later age may judge that more credit should go to the missionary on the harsh and uncompromising frontier than to the armchair critic sitting in his comfortable Swiss parsonage.

Sharply contrasted with the mission of Hebich, deeply rooted as it was in the pietism of southern Germany, was the highly confessional Lutheran Leipzig Mission, which entered the field in 1840. With the decline of the Danish Mission many of the old Lutheran congregations had been taken over by the Anglicans, on the whole without protest on the part of the Christians involved. In 1845 Tranquebar itself was acquired by the British from the Danes. The quiet waters were then disturbed by a great controversy on the subject of the observance of caste distinctions within the church. None of the churches had arrived at a clear policy on the matter. Robert de Nobili had treated it as a matter of social and not of religious concern, and had not made the abandonment of caste a condition of baptism. Later Roman Catholic missionaries had disliked caste, but had done little to eliminate it among Christians. Protestant missionaries had on the whole been more aware of caste as part of the religious system of Hinduism, and had felt that the refusal of full equality within the house of God was in itself a denial of the gospel, but they too had failed to convince the majority of Christians. Then the fourth bishop of Calcutta, Daniel Wilson (1833-58), an able and determined man, entered the controversy with a strongly worded pastoral letter in which he decreed that caste must be given up "decidedly, immediately and finally." The higher-caste Christians now in the Anglican fellowship were mortally offended; it was natural from their point of view that they should look for another home.

It was the Leipzig Mission that offered the new home. In 1844 Karl Graul became director of the mission, and before long issued directives in favor of a new policy. A strongly confessional Lutheran, he could regard only as aggression the methods by which the Anglicans seemed to be absorbing without limit the fruits of the old Lutheran work; he was prepared to make things easy for Lutherans who wished to return to their older tradition. Not content with directing the mission from Germany, Graul spent the years from 1849 to 1853 in India. During this period he not only learned the difficult Tamil language and produced a number of reliable translations of Tamil classics, but he also produced a number of writings on the theory and practice of missions, which give him some claim to be regarded as the founder of the science of missiology.

The list of bodies entering India in these years could be prolonged almost without end, to the weariness of the reader. Two further names must suffice. In 1841 the Irish Presbyterians, on the advice of John Wilson, entered Kathiawar, north of Bombay in western India, and a few years later took over Surat, the original home of the British in India, from the London Missionary Society. Many years later this small mission was to be adorned by Mrs. Sinclair Stevenson, the remarkable authoress of *Rites of the Twice-born,* a work which alone among missionary writings on Hindu lore can be compared with the *Manners and Customs of the Hindus* of the incomparable Abbé Dubois. In the very same year the Welsh Presbyterians moved into Assam, which had only recently been added to the British dominions, and set to work on the conversion of the people of the Khasi hills, thus inaugurating that work among the aborigines of India, which must occupy our attention in another connection.

MISSIONARY METHODS OF THE PERIOD

There was little difference in the missionary methods of the various Protestant missions of the time. It was taken for granted that the missionary would learn well the language of the area, and would become at least to some extent familiar with the customs of the people. A real interest in the non-Christian religions was rare — such knowledge as was acquired was mainly for controversial purposes. Bazaar and village preaching was carried out on a large scale, and sometimes with great effect. The distinguished scholar of Islam, C. G. Pfander, whose *Mizan-ul Haqq,* "Balance of Truth," is still a classic of the debate between Christianity and Islam, carried public disputation with the learned men of Islam to a very high level of competence, and won a number of converts by the excellence of his presentation of Christian truth. The work of Bible translation was carried forward, the old translations of Serampore being revised and versions in new languages being added to the list. Christian literature on a variety of themes was developed in a number of languages. Missionaries were so convinced of the absolute and exclusive truth of the Christian religion that their preaching was direct and uncompromising, and their hearers were presented with the obligation and responsibility of choice.

When converts were won, there was a tendency on the part of the missionaries to bring them in and to provide them with homes on the mission compound. Originally this had been a matter of necessity. No Christian could continue to live in a Hindu village; his wife, if she consented to remain with him, would not be allowed to draw water from the village well, and he and his family would have no part in the communal enterprises of the village. Except where, as in the south, group movements took place and a number of families entered the Christian church together, thus creating either a Christian village or a block too strong to be turned out by the Hindus, there was no way for the Christian to exist other than pulling up stakes and setting himself up afresh under the protection of the missionary. This seemed an excellent solution. The population at that time was comparatively small; the government was favorable and land was available. In area after area Christian villages grew up around the mission station, where the missionary became pastor, friend and guide in all the exigencies of life.

As time went on, what had been an emergency solution came to be accepted as a desirable solution. Would-be Christians were required by the missionaries to come and live in the Christian center, on the supposition that it would be impossible for them to live as true Christians in the non-Christian atmosphere of the village, and that the only way to Christian progress was total separation from the past. The Irish Presbyterians in particular worked out a plan of farm colonies, under which the Christians would live together in a measure of independence and prosperity; but even these colonies were kept under strict control of the missionary. Viewing the matter from the vantage point of later history we can see that here a grave mistake was made. These groups of Christians had no roots. Increasingly they became aliens in their own country, all the natural ramifications of family and community and caste having been lost. In almost every case the groups became sterile, having little opportunity to spread the Christian gospel, and in a number of cases little desire to share their new privileges with other people. Life in a non-Christian village was certainly hard, and the temptations provided by the Hindu atmosphere constant and difficult to resist. But unless it was absolutely impossible for the Christian to remain, it would have been better if he had stayed, endured hardship, and let his light shine among his non-Christian brethren. This mistaken choice of more than a hundred years ago was more responsible than anything else for the affirmation, so constantly heard today, that Christianity in India appears as a foreign religion.

THE THOMAS CHRISTIANS REAPPEAR

We left the Thomas Christians at the moment of the rebellion of the Koonen cross, and the separation of the Malankara from the Roman Catholic Church. It is now time to take up their story again.

Roman Catholics and Syrians lived together for a century and a half in uneasy juxtaposition, both in a state of great weakness. With the decline of the Portuguese power and the coming of the Dutch, the supply of priests, both foreign and indigenous, sank to a dangerously low level. The independent "Syrians" seem to have managed to maintain some contact with Mesopotamia, though it is likely that there were periods, perhaps long periods, during which they had no bishop. As far as Europe was concerned they were almost a forgotten people. Contact was resumed when the British took over Travancore as one of the Indian states under British protection and direction. The second resident, Colonel Munro, a man of strong Christian convictions, suggested to the Church Missionary Society that a mission of help should be sent, not to turn the Syrians into Anglicans, but to help in the training of the ministry and in the education of the people. His letters make it quite clear that he also entertained the hope that under wise teaching, the Syrians would learn to give up a number of "superstitions" which they had come to accept under Roman Catholic influence.

The British public had been informed of the existence of this ancient church through the *Christian Researches in Asia* of Claudius Buchanan, one of the "pious" chaplains, a remarkable man, who was expected by many to become the first bishop of Calcutta.[8] From the start a measure of illusion prevailed. Finding the Syrians strongly opposed to Rome, and free from what an evangelical Anglican regarded as the distortions of the Christian faith introduced by the Roman Catholics, Buchanan looked forward to an alliance between this ancient church and the Anglicans for the evangelization of India and the occupation of the field in advance of Roman Catholic propaganda. He, like many others after him, greatly underestimated the attachment of the people to their old ways, and overestimated their willingness to change those ways under the influence of European teaching.

---

[8] C. Buchanan, *Christian Researches in Asia; with notices of the Translation of the Scriptures into the Oriental Languages,* pp. 106-145.

What followed has become a matter of endless controversy, and it is still difficult to say exactly what happened. The mission of help arrived. It seems that the way had not been well prepared, and that from the start there were misunderstandings. Nevertheless, in 1816 Benjamin Bailey was able to establish himself in the seminary in Kottayam, to be followed later by Joseph Fenn and Henry Baker. The missionaries had been very strictly instructed to make no attempt to proselytize, and to make no changes without the authority of the Metropolitan Dionysius III. For a number of years excellent work was done. Up to this point the services had all been carried out in Syriac, hardly a word of which was intelligible to the people. Very little of the Bible existed in Malayalam, the local language. The missionaries succeeded in translating the whole Bible into Malayalam, and printing it on a press set up by Baker for that purpose. Affectionate relations grew up between the missionaries and their pupils, many of whom were destined for holy orders. It was hardly likely that this paradisal situation would continue. Naturally the missionaries worshipped among themselves according to the Anglican fashion — they were not communicants of the Syrian church. Through the reading of the Bible a number of the students became highly critical of a number of their own traditions, and were in the mood for a reformation. Younger missionaries who joined the staff were less prudent in their actions than their elders, and more violent in their denunciation of what they regarded as superstition. From 1835 onwards the new Metropolitan Dionysius IV became violently hostile to the missionaries, and a breach became inevitable.

The breach occurred in 1836. After that date the missionaries had no further direct contact with the church. Their work became educational, full freedom being maintained for Syrian students to attend what later became the Church Missionary Society College in Kottayam. Later, extensive evangelistic work among the Hindus led to a mass movement among the depressed class people of the area and to a considerable influx into the Anglican fold. In spite of these sensible arrangements, the very thing which was least desired and against which the missionaries had been ceaselessly warned came about, and a schism among the Syrians came into being. A number of them had become deeply attached to the simplicity of the Anglican service and were in revolt against a number of the inherited traditions. They could no longer feel at home in the ancient church, and maintained the position that, if the Church of England would not take them in, they would have no Christian home at all. The authorities of the Anglican Church were reluctant to agree, but in the end they consented. The number of those who withdrew from the ancient church was not large, but some of them were members of highly distinguished families. This group provided most of the leadership of what from 1879 to 1947 was the Anglican diocese of Travancore and Cochin, and produced the first Indian bishop of that diocese, C. K. Jacob.

ROMAN CATHOLICS RECOVER

In the first years of the nineteenth century the Roman Catholic Church had reached a low point from which, in the opinion of many, it would never be able to rise again. Religious apathy and uncertainty seemed to grow. France, for a hundred years the richest source of missionaries, had been desolated by the French Revolution and the dreadful period of the Napoleonic wars. Then the Concordat of 1801 between Napoleon and the churches, and the willingness of the Emperor to recreate in 1805 the three French missionary orders, provided that he kept these orders under control and used them in part at least for political purposes, gave some hope that the church was not finally to be suppressed. But the process of recovery was long and painful; after half a century of work the lost ground had hardly been made up.

The first step taken by Pius VII, after his release from French captivity and his return to Rome, was the reestablishment of the Society of Jesus, in direct defiance of the prohibition issued by his predecessor of 1773. Gradually the Jesuits returned to India and took up their forsaken work in the Tamil country and elsewhere. Other orders followed

— the Oblates of Mary Immaculate, the Salesians, the Carmelites and many others. But the work was still gravely hindered by the wretched quarrels arising out of the *Padroado,* the claim still maintained by the kings of Portugal that they alone had the right to nominate bishops for all the countries of the Far East. The Popes did not admit that this right extended beyond the territories actually under the control of the Portuguese, and sent out as their own representatives Vicars Apostolic for Madras (1832), for Calcutta (1834) and for Pondicherry (1836). The result was the so-called schism of Goa, in which the Portuguese refused to recognize the actions of the Pope and sent out to India bishops of their own choice without the approval of the Pope. In 1843 an attempt was made to heal the breach by the appointment of the learned, and it was believed conciliatory, Dr. Silva Torres to the see of Goa; but the plan collapsed when it was found that Torres, so far from making peace, came forward as a passionate supporter of the Portuguese cause. Yet the Pope would not allow himself to be thwarted in the carrying out of his plans. In 1858 there were sixteen vicariates in India, and the outlines of an ecclesiastical organization had come into existence.

Roman Catholicism had in the north one strange little enclave. Walter Reinhardt, a German, was typical of the unscrupulous adventurers of the day, who were prepared to serve under any master or none, provided that in the end they were able to carve out a kingdom for themselves. Reinhardt, having served under the French for some years, eventually received from the Mogul emperor Shah Alam the small princedom of Sardhana in the fertile Doab, which lies between the rivers Ganges and Jumna. He died in 1778, leaving behind him a young widow, a Muslim lady whom he had married in 1775. In 1781 the Begum Joanna Zebunissa Samru, as she came to be known, became a Roman Catholic, remaining faithful and becoming increasingly devout until her death in 1836. Through all the changes and chances of these fateful years the Begum managed to retain her principality, exercising friendship towards all, and large-hearted charity in which Anglicans and others were included no less than those of her own confession. In recognition of her piety the small city of Sardhana was raised to the status of a Vicariate Apostolic by Pope Gregory XVI. For fifty years Sardhana appeared as a kind of city of refuge to Christians who could not find a home elsewhere.

In northern India the strongest of the orders were the Capuchins. It was this order which produced the most notable of the Roman Catholic bishops of the period, Anastasius Hartmann, a Swiss of great ability and determination. Hartmann was for four years Vicar Apostolic of Patna, and was then transferred to Bombay, to take the lead in restoring peace and order after the troubles stirred up by the loyal adherents of the Padroado party. One of his main concerns was the status of Roman Catholic missions and clergy in India. The British government, though neutral between Hindus and Muslims, always tended to treat the Church of England in India as the state church. It was largely due to the efforts of Hartmann that this discrimination was modified, and Roman Catholic ecclesiastics were accorded the same recognition as those of the Anglican tradition.

It is interesting to observe that the battle for an Indian village priesthood was being fought out in the Roman Catholic Church exactly at the time that John Thomas was fighting a parallel battle among the Anglicans. In Goa there were too many priests, not all of the highest caliber; everywhere else there were far too few. But not much was being done to raise the number and to make possible the time when the missionary could withdraw in favor of Indian colleagues. The "image" of the priest was that of the missionary, master of a vast district over which he ruled paternally with a flock of obedient catechists under him. Little had been done by the Roman Catholics in the way of general education; the missionaries were of the opinion, perhaps rightly, that none of their Indian flock was capable of carrying these immense responsibilities. In 1841 a young Frenchman arrived in South India determined to change all this. Even before leaving France he had recorded it as the main purpose of his missionary venture "to direct all my own work and thought towards training a native clergy." Clearly Gaston de Marion Brésillac had powerful friends at court. In 1845, when he was only thirty-one, he was raised to the episcopate, and in 1850 became Vicár Apostolic of Coimbatore. But he had the utmost difficulty in making any impression on his colleagues. They were convinced that the Indian was incapable of rising to any high intellectual level, a strange blindness in a land so richly gifted in the field of intellect. And they had little understanding of Brésillac's idea of what an Indian priest should be. In his own words, "We must make sure not to expect them all to be missionaries. Some, no doubt, will be missionaries, but in the ordinary way it is enough that they be good priests charged with the care of a little parish." The rock of opinion remained immovable, and continued so until two popes of the twentieth century took vigorous action to make sure that the immovable was removed. Brésillac, concluding that for his time the struggle was in vain, resigned his post at the age of forty-two and returned to France. Later he was to lead the first Roman Catholic party to Sierra Leone, and to die within a few weeks of reaching the white man's grave.

THE END OF AN ERA

By 1850 the occupation of India, to use a somewhat outdated military term, had been completed in outline both on the Protestant and on the Roman Catholic side. The story we have told of new advance and of consolidation might suggest the measured advance of powerful armies. In point of fact, then as now, the striking force of the Christian churches was miserably small and inadequate to its task. In 1851 all the Protestant missions together had a missionary force of 339 ordained men; this meant a total force of about 600, including wives and other helpers. The Roman Catholic team was probably a little larger. On both sides the Indian ordained ministry was pitifully small; but there were large auxiliary forces on the catechist and teacher level. The service of women to women had hardly as yet begun. The Roman

Catholic numbers had by this time probably again reached the million mark. There may have been as many as 250,000 of the independent Thomas Christians. In 1851, the first year for which we have accurate figures, Protestant Christians were reckoned at 91,092, of whom the vast majority were in South India.

This may seem a very small cause to strike terror into the hearts of 150 million people. But there is no doubt that in the years after 1850 the rumor that the government was contemplating the forcible conversion of the country to Christianity had made considerable headway among the populace, and not least among the sepoys, the Indian soldiers on whom the Company mainly depended for the maintenance of order and the fighting of its wars. The causes of the Sepoy Rising of 1857 are many and complex and do not concern us here. In certain areas British rule had from the start been unpopular, and was of sufficiently recent origin for memories of another day to have survived vividly in the minds of many people. The researches of Indian historians, trained in the austere school of Western historical scholarship, have made it plain that the rising was not a national effort directed towards a future of independence, but the last stirring of the old spirit directed to the restoration of the past. As such it was from the start doomed to failure. The fighting was bitter, and many atrocities were committed on both sides. It does not appear that the malice of the mutineers was especially directed against missionaries or Christians as such — they were simply caught up in the fury of the times, and in a hostility which embraced all members of the white race and those Indians who were believed to be in league with them. It has been reckoned that thirty-six chaplains, missionaries and children perished, and a considerably larger number of Indian Christians.[9] But India as a whole failed to rise; the south remained entirely untouched by the events further north. It was not long before outward peace was restored, and the generous measures of conciliation adopted by the

9 The facts are set forth in detail in M. A. Sherring, *The Indian Church during the Great Rebellion.*

viceroy, "Clemency" Canning, helped to bring back the times of peace and ordered progress. But the effects of the rising were long-lasting and bitter on both sides. On one side the harm caused by the rising was that for a long time it injured the Indian "image" in Britain, , causing the Indian to be thought of as a childish and untrustworthy barbarian. On the other hand, deep and bitter memories of British barbarity remained for more than a generation ingrained in the minds of multitudes of Indians in the affected areas.

The rising had made it quite clear that the government of the East India Company must go. A trading company should never have been entrusted with the responsibility for the government of great dominions. Now that its failure to control a dangerous situation had been revealed, it must disappear, and must be replaced by the central government of Great Britain. The new situation and attitude were set forth in the famous proclamation of Queen Victoria, part of it certainly written by the monarch's own hand:

> Firmly relying ourselves on the truth of Christianity and acknowledging with gratitude the solace of religion, We declare it to be our royal will and pleasure that none be in any wise favoured, none molested or disquieted by reason of their religious faith or observances . . . and it is our further will that, so far as may be, our subjects of whatever race or creed, be freely and impartially admitted to offices in our service, the duties of which they may be qualified by their education, ability and integrity, duly to discharge.

This proclamation was intended to allay the anxieties and to soothe the nerves of Hindus and Muslims. Actually it served as a charter of religious liberty for the oppressed Indian Christian, whose right to life, liberty and the pursuit of happiness had never been recognized or guaranteed by the government of the East India Company. One age was dead; another was waiting to be born.

V

GREAT DAYS OF COLONIALISM

THE FIFTY YEARS WHICH FOLLOWED THE ASSUMPTION BY THE British crown of responsibility for the government of India were, for the greater part of the country, years of unbroken peace and of progress in many directions. The Indian Civil Service was reorganized on the basis of competition rather than patronage, and drew into itself a large number of remarkable and gifted men. There was as yet no question of admitting Indians into the higher ranks of the administration — this was the great period of colonialism and confidence in the wisdom of the Western powers. But a new standard not only of efficiency but of sympathetic and responsible administration was set up, a tradition of service to India which lasted until and beyond the declaration of the independence of India in 1947. Moreover, a large number of the new administrators — the Lawrences, Montgomery, James Monro — were devoted Christians, mostly of the evangelical persuasion, who had no hesitation about publicly confessing their faith; these, though scrupulously careful to maintain the government's policy of neutrality in all their public acts, stood side by side with the missionaries in all their efforts for the welfare of India, and believed that the gospel of Jesus Christ was itself the great instrument for the healing of the nations.

The first and greatest blessing that was brought to India in this time was unbroken peace. There were, of course, local disorders, but nothing that could be called a war. The visitor to the gigantic fortifications of Gingee in the south becomes aware of the change that has taken place; today the fortifications remain simply as a witness to a disturbed and combative past; they no longer serve any purpose, because there is no enemy against whom they could be used for the purposes of defense. It was mainly the peasants who profited by the new situation. They returned in large numbers to the land, now with secure titles of possession, and again took up the work of cultivation. Formerly barren areas were opened up through the first great dams, by which the waters of the rivers were made available for the irrigation of the fields.[1] Prices of grain tended to rise steadily. Population began to increase so rapidly that as early as 1881 the first hint was heard that overpopulation might come to be a danger.

After peace, the second great need of India was for rapid transportation. Without this, trade could not flourish, and the menace of famine could not be lifted. Though India had certain valuable mineral resources — especially coal, gold and manganese — and industrialization was gradually relieving the pressure of population on the soil, the greater number of people still depended on simple agriculture and therefore on the rainfall. Two successive years of failure of the monsoon meant hardship, and possibly death, for large numbers of people. The savior of India was the railway. The plans for a far-reaching railway system had already been laid in 1854 by Lord Dalhousie; by the end of the century the plan was in its essentials complete. The railways were laid

---

[1] The first of these great engineering works was completed before the change of government took place. The Ganges Canal, opened in 1854, according to the *Encyclopaedia Britannica* (10th ed., vol. 29, 1902, p. 599) "still holds its place unsurpassed among later irrigation works for boldness of design and completeness of execution."

out with care in such a way as to cross the most endangered areas, and to make possible the rapid transportation of grain to any area where shortage or famine might seem likely to occur. The last famine on the largest scale was that of 1877 in South India, by which old people were still dating their lives sixty years later, and which is vividly described in Rudyard Kipling's story, *William the Conqueror*.[2] Nothing on an equal scale occurred again till the great Bengal famine of 1943, which was brought about by entirely different causes, and the disastrous effects of which were greatly increased by the breakdown of local administration under wartime conditions. Under the famine code drawn up by the central government, local administrators received the most careful instructions as to the steps to be taken in case of failure of the rains. Together with relief, work on projects of public interest was to be arranged in order not merely that life should be preserved but also that those receiving help and food might not be pauperized. No greater service than this has ever been rendered by any colonial power to the people under its care.

When the administration of the East India Company was swept away, the last vestiges of its privileged monopoly of trade disappeared also. Free trade was now to be the rule. But since India was a poor country, the greater part of the capital through which trade and industry could be developed had to be provided from the West, and the Western pioneers claimed for themselves what later Indian opinion has reckoned as a ruinous share of the profits. It was observed that many of the mountainous or hilly areas of India provided a climate most suitable for the growing of tea. British enterprise developed the plantations, gave employment to many thousands of Indians, and opened up what is still one of India's most vigorous forms of trade. Certain areas of damp country in the east proved themselves ideally suited for the growing of jute; up to and beyond the first world war the world seemed to have an insatiable hunger for sacks

---

[2] And described in great detail in W. Digby, *The Famine Campaign in Southern India*, 2 vols.

of all kinds. Here it was the Scots who came in in force and made of India one of the greatest jute-producing countries in the world.[3] Before the end of the century, however, the Western monopoly was beginning to be challenged. When the great iron and steel works of Jamshedpur came into being, though many of the managers were European, the owners and directors belonged to the great Parsi family of the Tatas.

One unplanned consequence of the *laissez faire* policy worked gravely to the detriment of India. The Indian market was opened to the cheap textiles of Lancashire, and the great Indian tradition of weaving was seriously undermined, since only at certain points could hand-woven cloth compete with that manufactured by the West. The aim of the free trade principle was the best advantage of all; but, as so often happens when a theory is applied in all circumstances without regard to difference of needs, grave harm was done. India exported its cotton to Britain and received it back in the form of finished cloth, instead of retaining it at home to make for itself the cloth which it needed. This policy, and the failure to introduce a measure of protection for Indian crafts and industries, caused much bitterness, and was the darker side of imperial rule during what was in the main a period of rapid and unimpeded progress.

IN DIVERSE FORMS AND MANY FASHIONS

Progress in political and economic affairs was accompanied by unparalleled progress in missionary work.

Here what strikes the observer first is the extraordinary diversification of Christian work. Of course the preaching of the gospel still held first place; but the churches were discovering the great variety of ways in which the gospel could be preached.

Up to 1858 missionary work had been regarded primarily as work for men; between 1858 and 1908 the number of women engaged in missionary work came greatly to exceed

---

[3] Indigo, the third of the great revenue-producing crops of India, was ruined when in 1897 a German firm placed synthetic indigo on the market.

the number of men. Before 1858 the unmarried woman in the
field was hardly known. It was not regarded as safe for European women to live unprotected by men in what was still
a disturbed and unruly land. And, as the unsympathetic
bishop Daniel Wilson remarked, "If you send them out, they
will all be married off within the year." Gradually the objections were overruled, and the unmarried woman missionary became a regularly recognized part of the missionary
scene.

In certain cases special missionary societies were organized
for women. The Zenana Bible and Medical Mission grew
out of a body with the typical Victorian title, "The Indian
Female Normal School and Institution Society." The Church
of England Zenana Missionary Society was formed in 1880.
As the names imply, much of the work of these groups con-
sisted of the visiting of Indian women in their homes. *Purdah* is not as strictly observed in India as in some other
countries; but it was simply a fact that Hindu and Muslim
women of high caste were practically inaccessible except in
their homes, and that the vast majority of them were illiterate. Regular visits from the missionaries and from the
Biblewomen under their direction brought light and interest
into the lives of many thousands of these women, and in a
number of cases led them to a sincere and simple faith in
Christ. This was a quiet and little noted work, and many
of those who believed could not be baptized, since the consequence would have been immediate ejection from their
homes.[4]

From the beginning the missions had been pioneers in the
education of women and girls. In the early days missionaries
had been so determined that girls as well as boys should learn
to read that they had actually paid the parents in compensation for the loss of the girls' labor at home which would
result from their coming to school. It was not long, however,

---

[4] I have just come across an unsigned article in the missionary review
The East and the West for 1905 (pp. 241-244) entitled "Baptism within
the Purdah," and raising the question whether high-caste women converts could not be baptized by duly ordained deaconesses in their homes.

before Christians became aware of the advantage of having
educated daughters, to be followed by Hindus, and at a much
slower pace by Muslims. The number of girls' schools increased rapidly after 1858. One of the notable names in this
connection is that of the American Isabella Thoburn, who
arrived in 1870, and founded in Lucknow a school that was
destined to grow into a college which still bears her name.
Another school which also grew into a college was the Sarah
Tucker school in Palamcottah in the far south, flanked by
two other pioneer schools, one for the deaf and one for the
blind.

It was, however, no missionary but an Indian woman who
first made known to the entire world the needs of the Indian
woman for education, and the capacities that were latent in
the Indian woman herself, if she were set free to serve her
own people in the name of Christ. The career of Pandita
Ramābai was wholly exceptional. Born in a Brahman family,
she was the daughter of an unusual man who believed that
girls should have the same educational opportunities as boys.
She became deeply versed in all the wisdom of the ancient
world of India. Left a widow with one small daughter, in
1882 she made her way to England, and while there became
convinced of the truth of the Christian faith and was baptized. On her return to India she gave herself to the service
of the child widows, who, betrothed as infants, were left as
widows with no opportunity of marrying again by the death
of a husband they had hardly seen. To this cause was later
added that of orphans from the famine of 1895-96 in western
India. Ramābai's institution of Mukti (deliverance) gradually grew into an immense complex of teaching, industry,
(dairy-farming, weaving, rope-making and so on), and worship at the center of which stood the frail figure of the Pandita
herself until her death in 1922. She herself would have attributed all her achievements to the Christ in whom she
had come to trust, and who, as she most firmly believed,
dwelt in her to carry out his own work of compassion.

A second area of extension was that of medical missions.
Reference has already been made to the Scudders and the

beginning of medical work in the south; but this had been little more than incidental, on the margin of missionary work properly so called. It was after 1858 that the missions came to see the value of medical work as a means of opening up access to the people in areas where for one reason or another they were particularly unapproachable. The Church Missionary Society developed a whole range of hospitals along the northwest frontier, at Dera Ghazi Khan (1876), Quetta (1885) and other centers. In 1892 Theodore Pennell, a man marked by a singular purity and humility of life, found his sphere of service at Bannu; to be followed by the far more famous eye-surgeon, Sir Henry Holland, whose name was to be a legend on the frontier for the best part of sixty years. But it was not only in such remote and difficult areas that tht churches saw the work of healing as part of the Christian ministry to the whole man. At an early date (1854) the London Missionary Society had opened at Neyyoor in Travancore a hospital which was later to grow into one of the largest in India; for a number of years they secured the services of T. H. Somervell, the Everest climber. Fifty miles from Calcutta, in a densely populated and malaria-ridden region, James Monro, the former Indian civilian, founded in 1892 with the help of his doctor son and son-in-law the Ranaghat Medical Mission, which at its hospital Doyabari, "the House of Mercy," built up an astonishing record of service, though with few conversions.

The early doctors had all been men, for the simple reason that even in the West women were not being trained as doctors. Here it was America that first broke through the ancient prejudice and opened its medical halls to women as well as to men. In consequence it was an American society, that of the American Methodists, which had the honor of sending the first fully qualified woman doctor to India. Clara Swain arrived in India in 1870, and opened her first hospital for women at Bareilly in Uttar Pradesh in 1874. She was followed in the next year by Sara Seward, sent out by the American Presbyterians to Allahabad. Before long the medical women realized that their work must as soon as possible be supplemented by Indian women doctors, since the immense need could not be met by foreign workers. A small beginning was made as early as 1881 with the Medical Missions Training Institute of the United Presbyterian Mission, started at Agra by Dr. Valentine. This was not so much an independent institution as a supplement to the training given in the government school of medicine. Much more ambitious was the North India School of Medicine started for Christian women at Ludhiana by Dr. Edith Brown in 1894. This was to be a fully equipped training center, preparing both doctors and nurses for the government medical examinations.

In the south Dr. Ida Scudder was led to start at Vellore a pioneer institution for the training of women doctors. In later times both Ludhiana and Vellore branched out to supply training for men as well as for women, in the belief that only medical training based on the Christian understanding of man is adequate preparation for the service that the doctor is called to render to his fellow men.

In industrial missions the Basel Mission still held pride of place. Many other enterprises, industrial and agricultural, were set up, with the laudable intention of making the poor Christians economically independent of the missions and able to support themselves. Such undertakings are exceedingly difficult and very expensive to run. Many of the mission enterprises were amateurish and not highly effective. An exception must be made in favor of the Agricultural Institute at Allahabad, founded in 1910 by Dr. Sam Higginbottom. Here the resources of a number of missions, combined with the special help received from the Rockefeller and other foundations in America, made it possible for the missions to create an institution which could bear comparison with any other in the country, training students up to the highest levels of competence in agricultural science, but never forgetting that India is a land of villages, and bearing always in mind that the Christian farmer knows himself to be a fellow worker with the Lord of all lands.

NEW FORCES AT WORK

During the period between 1850 and 1914 a great many Protestant missionary societies entered India.

The largest of these new societies was the American Methodist Episcopal Church, the first representative of which reached India in 1856. Over the next thirty-five years this society opened with bewildering rapidity a series of stations, mainly in the north at such centers as Lucknow, Kanpur and Bareilly; but Karachi in Sind was opened up in 1874, Baroda in Gujerat in 1888, Nagpur in central India in 1876; and as early as 1873 Hyderabad in the dominions of the Nizam. By 1890 the Methodists had in India ninety ordained missionaries, thus surpassing all the other Protestant missions with the single exception of the Church Missionary Society. The Methodists gave themselves to rapid and extensive evangelization, and soon found themselves involved in one of the main missionary controversies of the nineteenth century: at what stage of Christian conviction should baptism be given? The Roman Catholics had on occasion baptized inquirers with hardly any preparation whatsoever; the majority of the Protestant societies had come to insist on a long period of preparation and testing, baptism being the expression of a well-rooted and considered Christian faith. The Methodists took the view that baptism should be given at a very early stage — first baptize and then Christianize. There were dangers in both directions. If baptism was too long delayed, candidates tended to become discouraged and to drift away from the Christian cause; if early baptism could not be followed by thorough Christian instruction, the mission was likely to find itself with a mass of baptized heathenism on its hands.

The Lutherans extended themselves in various directions. Mention may be made of the Danish Mission which came in in 1861, took over the South Arcot District, and worked with exemplary thoroughness and patience though without reward of any large number of believers. American Lutherans worked further north in the Telugu area. In 1894 a number of the younger Lutheran missionaries, dissatisfied with what seemed to them laxity in dogmatic teaching, turned to the rigidly confessional Missouri Synod in the United States, which came in and set up a number of stations in the Tamil area of the Madras presidency and in Travancore. This mission showed less regard than most for the principle that one Protestant mission was not to set up work in an area in which another mission was already present. Its ecumenical awakening took place only in the second half of the twentieth century.

The Salvation Army began its Indian work in 1883 with a sense of universal mission to the deprived and underprivileged. Among its notable early leaders was the former member of the Indian Civil Service, Commissioner Frederick Booth-Tucker. The early Salvationists believed that other missionaries had lived far too comfortable lives; they would wear Indian dress and go almost to the limit in identifying themselves with the poverty of those to whom they had come to minister. Many died. The heroic adventure proved itself to be more exacting than Western flesh and blood could endure in the Indian climate. A less exacting form of life had to be adopted. Nevertheless, it remains true that many workers of the Salvation Army accepted standards of living that would have frightened the majority of missionaries away. They rendered especially excellent service among the criminal tribes, of which there were many in India, and whose nomadic habits have caused perplexity to every Indian government.

THE GOSPEL FOR THE ABORIGINES

From time to time missionaries had found themselves in contact with some of the pre-Dravidian peoples, who had been driven away into the hills and jungles by stronger invaders. Some of these remote tribes could be numbered in the hundreds. Others were powerful peoples, like the Santals, with their own clearly marked traditions and perhaps three million members. Over the centuries some of these peoples have been increasingly assimilated by their Hindu neighbors, but few have been entirely incorporated into the Hindu system. This separateness has rendered them especially accessible to the Christian message.

One of the first missions to begin working among such people on a large scale was the Gossner Mission in Chota Nagpur. This society had started in the great Ganges plain, and had worked with the same lack of success as others. About 1848 the attention of the missionaries was drawn to the Kolarian people of the fertile upland of Chota Nagpur. Here a number of peoples, Oraons, Hos and Mundas, lived together in a world of their own. But it was a threatened world; Bengalis, of higher education and greater knowledge of the world, were pressing in, and the aborigines felt themselves threatened, both in their way of life and in the possession of their lands. To them the British appeared as the protectors; the belief that the missionaries were approved by the ruling powers helped to give them status in the eyes of the people. The first baptisms took place in 1850. From that time on one station after another was founded. Converts began to come in, so that in 1863 the number of the baptized had risen to 3,401. Careful instruction was the rule, and, through the introduction of an excellent system of village elders, from an early stage the people themselves were introduced to responsibility for the maintenance and development of the Christian life among them. On these well-laid foundations a powerful church grew up. After a century of work the fully independent Lutheran Church of Chota Nagpur and Assam was a powerful body with more than 200,000 baptized members.

No more in this area, however, than in others, did the course of Christian progress run smooth. In 1869 a serious difference of opinion broke out between the old missionaries who had borne the burden and heat of the day and the younger forces recently arrived from Germany. After various attempts at compromise the older men, finding the situation intolerable, turned to Bishop Milman of Calcutta and asked for Anglican ordination and for a home in a church which they thought would better care for the needs of the situation. They believed that their entire flock would follow them. In this they were deceived; the majority stayed within the Lutheran fold. But those who did move out, about one-third of the whole, came to form the nucleus of the Anglican diocese of Chota Nagpur, which at the time of writing has its first bishop of Kolarian stock, Hans Dilbar.

Far more serious for the Lutherans was the entry of the Jesuits into their chosen preserve. The success of this new mission was small, until a tremendous wave was set in motion by the arrival of a Flemish Jesuit Constant Lievens. This remarkable man, realizing the distress of the Kols under the steadily increasing oppression from without, set himself at their head in a campaign of disobedience to the unjust demands of the landholders and their agents. Enthusiasm knew no limits. Many Lutherans and Anglicans fell away to the Roman Catholics, though far fewer than Lievens claimed. The methods used were not always highly scrupulous; the motives of the candidates for baptism had little to do with the Christian faith. Nevertheless it remains a fact that in the year 1891, in which Lievens after only six years in India had to return exhausted to Belgium, the Roman Catholics already had a church of 73,623 converts. With the withdrawal of Lievens, methods became more normal; the wild agitation among the Kols died away, and order was restored. But the Roman Catholic Church still has in the area a larger number of Christians than the Anglicans and the Lutherans put together.

Various missions have worked among the Santals, on the border between Bengal and Bihar. Among these was the Santal Mission of the Northern Churches, founded in 1867 by the Norwegian L. O. Skrefsrud and the Dane H. P. Børresen. Skrefsrud was a remarkable man, who in his youth had spent four years in prison and had there come to a profound evangelical conversion. He proved to be a linguist of more than ordinary capacity, and produced a grammar of the Santal language which is still in general use. It was the aim of Skrefsrud as far as possible to keep the Christians within the limits of their own tribal traditions, changing only those things which were unmistakably contrary to their Christian profession. On his few furloughs in the West, Skrefsrud gave evidence of astonishing gifts as a preacher of revival.

The Khonds, a Dravidian people in Orissa, have found a
place in all the books on anthropology because of their
well-established custom of human sacrifice. The aim of the
sacrifice was clearly to exercise a powerful magic which
would secure and increase the fertility of the fields. The
Meriah, who must belong to another tribe, was kindly treated
until the moment of the sacrifice, and then painlessly killed;
his body was cut in fragments and scattered through the
fields.[5] Roman Catholic missionaries were at work among
these interesting people from 1850 onwards. The American
Baptists came up from the plains at a rather later date.
Work was difficult, owing to the nomadic habits of the people,
but several thousands have become Christians.

Faithful work has been carried on among two large peoples
of central India, the Gonds in the area of Kipling's *Jungle
Books,* and the Bhils, but without bringing into existence
large and permanent churches. Much greater success attended
the work of the Welsh Presbyterians, who, as we saw, climbed
up into the Khasi hills in 1842, and after fifty years of work
had 189 churches and over 2,000 communicants. Similar success attended the English Baptists when they moved up from
the plains of Bengal to the Lushai hills. The American Baptists pressed even further into the land of the head-hunting
Nāgas, that still-disputed area between India, Burma and
China where the people have striven to maintain their own
independence against the centralized government of India.
The success among many tribes has been such that whole
areas have been transformed from primitive animism to
orderly Christian existence.

The Todas, a very ancient Dravidian tribe living 7,000 feet
above sea level in the Nilgiri hills, are among the smallest
peoples in the world. When the Europeans discovered them
there were perhaps a thousand of them, pasturing their buf-
faloes on the high slopes and regarding themselves as the
kings of all creation. But, in contact with a higher civilization
and the sicknesses which it brought, the number dwindled to

---

5 The practice of human sacrifice was suppressed by vigorous action on
the part of the British government in India between 1847 and 1854.

600 and seemed likely to sink still further. At this point Miss
Catherine Ling, who had come to India in 1881 at the age
of 20, began to be interested in this small and neglected
people. The first baptism took place in 1903, and from that
time on a small Toda Christian community began to come
into being. The Toda Christians present an interesting problem for ethnologists. In spite of strenuous government efforts to preserve them, the non-Christian Todas are only just
beginning to recover from a long period of decline; the Christian Todas have on an average six children per family, and
are thriving and multiplying. What is it in the gospel that
gives new life and power of survival to so gravely threatened
a people?

THE GOSPEL FOR THE OUTCASTES

We have earlier commented on the extraordinary stability
given to Indian society by the caste system. But for this stability a heavy price had to be paid, in that it rested on a
basis of exclusion, and that at the bottom of the pyramid
were to be found multitudes, almost one-fifth of the population, who were barred from all social privilege and existed
in extreme poverty and degradation. These represent, in all
probability, the pre-Dravidian element in the population which
was reduced by stronger invaders to an almost servile status.
A great many of them are landless laborers; others per-
form what are regarded by the Hindus as menial or de-
grading occupations, such as drummers, leather-workers, scav-
engers and so forth. The Hindu doctrine of caste, according
to which a man's status in this life indicates the measure
of his guilt or virtue in previous lives, is called in to justify
the system; the outcaste cannot change his lot in this life,
but he may hope to better it in another birth by faithful
fulfillment of the duties to which he is called in his present
phase of existence. The government of independent India
has legally abolished untouchability, but in the villages
things are slow to change, and a better way of life is only
very slowly opening out before the eyes of the members of

the "scheduled and backward" castes, as it is now reckoned to be more polite to call them.

The attention of the missionaries had been drawn to these people from an early date, but little serious attempt had been made to win them for the church. Some missions had their hands full with movements among the poor but slightly more privileged castes. The majority of missionaries directed their efforts first to the high-caste people, in the expectation that, if they were converted, through their witness the gospel would rapidly spread downwards to the less fortunate strata of society. The great movements among the "outcastes" began only a century ago, to a large extent unsought and undesired by the missionaries.

The first notable movement began in the Telugu area north of Madras, when in 1877 John E. Clough of the American Baptist Mission found himself confronted with a group of 200 people of the Madiga caste, who had believed in Jesus through the preaching of a man of their own community and were now asking for baptism. This man, Yerraguntla Periah, had been in touch with Anglican missionaries, and had passed on to his relations all that he knew of the gospel. The Christian movement was the result of his work. At first Dr. Clough was very doubtful of the rightness of baptizing such a group, since he was imbued with the then prevailing philosophy of missions that new Christians could not live a Christian life in their own villages. Eventually he was prevailed upon to grant baptism; within a few years he found himself with a movement on his hands so widespread that within five years more than twenty thousand people had been baptized. The movement continued to grow and to spread among the two main groups of the depressed classes in the area, the Mālas and the Mādigas. All the missions profited and more than a million people were added to the church in thirty years.

A rather similar process began far away in the Sialkot district of the Punjab. Here the work began with the conversion of a small, dark, lame Chuhra named Ditt; there occurred the same desire to remain among his own people, the same hesitancy on the part of the missionaries, the same final acceptance, and again the beginning of a large movement. Between 1870 and 1914 the greater part of the Chuhra community in that area had been brought into the church.

This strange phenomenon of the mass movement attracted much attention and rather varied comment. One of the great protagonists of such movements was Henry Whitehead, brother of the philosopher A. N. Whitehead, and from 1899 till 1923 bishop of Madras. Whitehead was convinced that such movements were valid manifestations of the working of the Spirit of God, and that, though a high standard of personal faith was not to be expected of every convert from the beginning, a door was open through which the church must at all costs enter. He believed, not without reason, that, given the necessary supply of Christian workers, thirty million people of the depressed classes could be gathered into the church within a century. Most of the Indian leaders of the church and many of the missionaries took the opposite view. By great efforts the Indian Christian church had been raised to a high level of literacy and social acceptance. If it were flooded with thousands of the illiterate and depraved, all that had been accomplished would be undone, and Christianity would be associated to its great detriment only with the poorest and least acceptable classes of society.

Both views continue to be held. But gradually the majority of missionaries came to accept the mass movements, with all their problems, as an opening for the gospel given by God himself. Outcaste converts had in many places shown their ability to stand fast in face of persecution. The change in social conditions as a result of Christian conversion was in many cases so startling as to lead to inquiry on the part of high-caste Hindus as to the power which had effected so rapid and beneficial a transformation. Educational effort showed that the children of the outcastes were not innately inferior in intelligence to those of other communities, though their progress was often hindered by malnutrition and extreme poverty. The Methodist bishop J. W. Pickett, in two remarkable books, *Christian Mass Movements in India* (1933)

and *Christ's Way to India's Heart* (1938), analyzed the movements, and showed that for people on this level of existence
corporate rather than individual decision was the natural
approach.

The mass movements did not fulfill the worst fears of their
critics or the highest hopes of their supporters. In no case
was the supply of workers, foreign and indigenous, adequate
to the demands made by hundreds of groups of new Christians. All workers in this field had to bewail the lack of
quality and conviction in the third generation. In area after
area a promising movement, having reached its peak within
a few years, gradually lost impetus and sank back into slow
and hardly remarkable progress. Nevertheless, it remains
true that the vast majority of Indian Christians today are of
depressed class or animistic origin.

THE THOMAS CHRISTIANS AGAIN

We left the Church of the Thomas Christians in a state
of tension between the well-intentioned efforts of reforming
missionaries and the strict adherence to tradition of a not
very friendly Metropolitan.

· Though a small minority of Syrians had seceded to the
Church of England, the majority remained true to the old
allegiance, and the situation appeared to be calm. But be-
neath the surface the reforming leaven continued to work,
the leader in the movement being Abraham Malpan, the
Syriac teacher in the seminary at Kottayam. This outstanding
man had no intention of leaving the church in which he had
been born, or of creating division within it; but he saw more
clearly than many others the need for reform in the light
of the new biblical knowledge which had been brought and
disseminated by the missionaries. His position in the seminary gave him great influence, especially among the younger
clergy. With a view to strengthening his position, Abraham
took the shrewd step of sending his nephew, Matthew Athanasius, to visit the Syrian Patriarch at Mardin in Syria. In 1843
Matthew returned to India as bishop and Metran for the
Syrian church. He was not readily received by all, but by

1852 he had managed to eject all rivals, and remained un-
troubled in his office until 1865. It seems certain that Matthew
shared his uncle's reforming principles, but he was cautious
in advocating change, and he secured the loyalty of a majority
of his people. But in 1865 the malcontents dispatched Pulikot
Joseph to the Patriarch, with the request that he be consecrated and sent back to India as Metran. This led to fourteen
years of bitter disputes between Matthew and Dionysius V,
as Pulikot Joseph now styled himself. A personal visit of
the Patriarch to India from 1875 to 1877 immensely strength-
ened the hands of Dionysius and the conservative party, and
also established a domination of the Patriarch over the
church such as had never been known before. The death of
Matthew in 1877 did not clear up the situation, since his
successor, Mar Thomas Athanasius, had already been consecrated.

In 1879 the climax of the dispute was reached. As a result
of extended lawsuits, the entire property of the church was
given to the conservative party, and Thomas Athanasius and
his followers were left with nothing. At one moment the
reforming group was inclined to follow the example of an
earlier schism and to become Anglicans. But wise friends on
the Anglican side urged them to organize themselves as an
independent Eastern church; they had a regularly consecrated
bishop, and there were therefore no difficulties, from the
point of view of church order, in the way of this procedure.
So the Mar Thoma Syrian Church came into being. With a
membership of about 200,000, it was considerably smaller
than either the Roman Catholic or Malankara sections of the
church; but it has held together, combining many of the
ancient traditions of the church with a simple biblical
theology, and it has been distinguished by notable evangelistic zeal, both within its homeland of Kerala and far
beyond.

The division of the two parties into two churches did not
bring peace to the conservatives. Their unity was threatened
by deep-seated differences of opinion as to the rights of the
Patriarch and the relative independence of the Indian church.

More than two generations were to pass before this strife was healed. This section of the church, much weakened by these contentions and a number of secessions to Rome resulting from them, has received much help from the Anglo-catholic wing of the Anglican Church, and especially from the Oxford Mission to Calcutta.

ROMAN CATHOLIC PROGRESS

By the middle of the nineteenth century Roman Catholic work in India was beginning to recover strength and tone. But a thorough visitation of the whole of India, carried out between 1858 and 1862 by two devoted French bishops, Mgr. Bonnand of Pondicherry and Mgr. Charbonneaux of Mysore, followed by a lengthy report, offers us a clear picture of the grave weaknesses under which the work suffered at this time. The most serious defect was the almost total lack of an indigenous clergy. In seven vicariates — Vizagapatam, Hyderabad, Dacca, Calcutta, Bombay, Patna and Agra — not a single Indian priest was to be found. In six others there was no seminary. Only in the Roman Catholic section of the Thomas Christians was the supply of priests adequate; but here quantity was not matched by quality, and 10 per cent of the priests were under suspension for a variety of offenses. Although new orders continued to come in, and the work of priests was being increasingly supplemented by that of nuns and sisters, the total missionary force was far too small to undertake the evangelization of India on a major scale. And such forces as there were, were weakened by the never-ending disputes between those of Portuguese allegiance and those more directly related to Rome.

Rome acts slowly, but in the end it acts decisively. At last in 1886 Pope Leo XIII decided that this unsatisfactory system must exist no longer, and that a regular hierarchy must be established. The Archbishop of Goa was to receive the rather meaningless title of Patriarch of the East, and certain privileges were still reserved to the Portuguese government in connection with certain sees. Otherwise, a diocesan hierarchy would be established, and bishops would take their titles from Indian cities and not from obscure villages in North Africa. Seven ecclesiastical provinces were created — Goa, Pondicherry, Verapoly, Madras, Calcutta, Agra and Bombay. To complete the structure the Pope appointed an Italian prelate, Mgr. Agliardi, as Apostolic Delegate and as his personal representative for India and Ceylon. Bishops had now been supplied in adequate numbers; but every single one of them was a foreigner. This was not surprising, in the light of what has been said about the defects of the Indian clergy; it seems to have been simply taken for granted by everyone that an Indian episcopate was a dream for a very distant future. In 1896 Pope Leo XIII took the first step to correct this undesirable situation. In that year special arrangements were made for the spiritual oversight of the Roman Catholic branch of the Thomas Christians; for each of three dioceses an Indian priest from the ranks of the ancient church was appointed bishop. This area was placed not under the Propaganda but under the Congregation for the Oriental churches. The first consecration of a bishop of the Latin rite took place after the end of the period which is dealt with in this chapter.

The need for an indigenous clergy was now evident to everyone with the exception of a number of old-fashioned missionaries. But a ministry cannot be created out of nothing; it can develop only where there is an educated laity, out of which candidates for the priesthood will come forward. Till the middle of the century the Roman Catholic missions had done little for education. Schools were fewer than those of the Protestants, and mostly of inferior quality. There were hardly any institutions for higher learning, and no seminary of first-rate quality. Within half a century this situation was radically changed.

The moment was propitious. Even before the imperial government took over responsibility for the affairs of India, the attention of the authorities had been directed to the problem of education.[6] No attempt was made to develop a

---

[6] The famous dispatch of Sir Charles Wood, President of the Board of

national system of education under government control. An ingenious plan was worked out, under which the government undertook to give financial aid to any group, religious or secular, or indeed in certain cases to individuals, who were prepared to run schools on lines approved by the education department, accepting certain conditions with regard to standards, methods, and curriculum and regular inspection by a representative of the department. No obstacle was placed by the authorities in the way of religious instruction in state-aided schools. The opportunity was open to everyone. Far more than any other group the missions saw their opportunity; the network of schools was rapidly extended, in some areas all the schools being Christian schools of one denomination or another. Roman Catholics started later, and did not reach the same level as the other missions until the middle of the twentieth century; but their progress was proportionately more rapid. In early days some missions had been inclined to provide education for Christian children only; the great majority, however, were willing to educate all comers, and where religious instruction was well carried out, the schools became one of the main sources of converts for the churches.

Not content with its efforts for the schools, the British government proceeded to establish five universities to educate Indian students up to the level of universities in the West, and thus to provide that educated Indian elite upon which the government would more and more come to rely.[7] These universities were to work on the federal principle of the University of London; thus it was possible for colleges at a distance from the center to become a part of the university, one of the main functions of which was the holding of examinations and the granting of degrees. In course of

Control, on the Education of India, was dated 19 July 1854. But for ten years little was done to implement its recommendations.

[7] The University of Calcutta was founded in 1857. Those of Bombay, Madras, Lahore and Allahabad were added in the course of the next thirty years.

time all the existing Protestant colleges became integrated with the new universities.

The Protestants had been first in the field of higher education. In the second half of the century Roman Catholics also saw the opportunity and entered in. Some small attempts had been made at founding colleges for Europeans in the main centers of the French and Portuguese dominions. The first university college for Indians appears to have been founded, or refounded, in Calcutta by the Belgian Jesuits in 1860; this college of St. Francis Xavier, after a series of strange vicissitudes, now has behind it more than a century of successful work. A young Swiss bishop, Alexis Canoz, had attempted in 1844 to open a college at Negapatam in southeast India; this first attempt was brought to an abrupt end through the hostility of the Goanese faction, who succeeded in burning down the college building. A second attempt at Trichinopoly in 1883, under the guidance of the same enterprising bishop, was more successful; St. Joseph's College is now one of the largest in India. Within a comparatively brief time colleges had come into existence in Bombay, in Madras, in Palamcottah, and a dozen other centers. The great majority of students were non-Christian; but the foundation had been laid upon which within a century the fully developed structure of the Indian priesthood and episcopate would arise.

BALANCE OF A CENTURY

If numbers are taken as a criterion, the success of the Christian missions between 1814 and 1914 must be held to have been considerable. There had been many setbacks, but each time of depression had in the end been followed by a time of advance. Accurate statistics are hard to come by, but it seems that in 1914 the Christians in the whole of India numbered about three and a half million. Of these nearly two-thirds were Roman Catholic, 10 per cent Christians of the independent Syrian churches, and about a quarter Protestant. The Roman Catholics had quadrupled their number in a century. Proportionately the progress of the Protestants had been much more rapid; since starting from almost nothing at the beginning of the nineteenth century, they had multiplied themselves eight times over in the years between 1858 and 1914. Christians were, however, very unevenly distributed. In some areas of the south they were so numerous as to produce on the mind of a visitor almost the impression of being in a Christian country. In many areas Christians were a tiny minority. In yet others nothing had been done at all, either because, as in Rewa, one of the larger Indian native states, the Hindu ruler forbade all Christian propaganda in his area, or because the always slender Christian forces had not found it possible to penetrate so far.

The great majority of Christians were of poor and humble origin. Every year was marked by the conversion of some Muslims, and of some from the highest Hindu castes. But these were always few; the penalty of total exclusion from the family and from every association with the past made baptism difficult for many, especially women, who under easier conditions might have been willing openly to follow Christ. And one of the main sources of such conversions, the colleges, had been drying up. As the ancient religions rallied their forces and re-interpreted their teaching, an increasing number of students found it possible to go a long way in the acceptance of the teaching of Jesus without taking the radical steps of public confession and baptism. To some missionaries this was a disappointment; others, such as William Miller, the great principal of the Christian college in Madras from 1862 to 1907, rationalized the situation, and declared that the aim of the colleges was not to separate individuals from the mass, but to carry on a process of fermentation, of penetration of the whole non-Christian world by the message of the gospel, with a view to a great ingathering at some future date. From about 1870 on the colleges performed their greatest service not so much as evangelistic instruments as in training that highly educated Christian elite, without which it is impossible that the church can flourish. To many this will seem a sufficient justification for their existence.

The weakness of the Indian church was its foreignness.

For this, as we have seen, the missionaries were less to blame than has sometimes been supposed. Yet almost all the leading positions in all the churches were held by foreigners. A certain amount of pressure was undoubtedly exercised on Indians to adopt foreign ways. And more perhaps than they themselves realized, the missionaries had come to lean on the strong arm of the colonial government. They appreciated the peace and order that it had brought, and the many forms of help that it was prepared to render to every form of social service. This did not so greatly matter in the high days of colonialism, when the majority of the Indian people were content with a government which, though foreign, was on the whole just and in many ways progressive. But there was bound to be trouble, if at any time an Indian national movement were to arise. Prejudice against the foreign government would almost certainly be reflected in prejudice against the foreign religion. Missionaries and government officials both made the mistake of coming to regard themselves as permanent. They failed to see how rapidly the tides of history were setting in an entirely different direction, and to realize how ill-prepared the church was to adapt itself to the changed situation, which within the course of a few years it was going to have to face.[8]

---

[8] There is reason to think that the church in India became more, rather than less, foreign in appearance as it increased in numbers. This was in part due to the great increase in the number of missionaries after 1858; but, until much more research has been done on the subject, it will not be possible to speak with confidence on the causes of this remarkable change.

VI

THE INDIAN REACTION

THE OTHER END OF THE TELESCOPE

WE USUALLY SEE MISSIONARY WORK THROUGH THE EYES OF THE missionaries. Inevitably they tend to magnify their office and to give as favorable a report as possible on their doings. For this reason all missionary writing must be critically handled by the serious historian, and it is good sometimes to turn the telescope the other way, to see the missionaries through the eyes of those who are the objects, or as some would say, the victims of their operations.

This is by no means easy to do. We have, indeed, many pictures of missionaries and their work from the pens of other Europeans — traders, officials, and tourists — and these are often sharply critical and even hostile. Valuable as these may be as a corrective, they do not give us what we want: the Indian reaction to the message of the gospel. From the time of Robert de Nobili on, missionaries have left accounts of their discussions and controversies with non-Christians; but these are naturally recorded in the missionary's own words and give his impression of what took place; it is never certain that he fully understood what was meant by his interlocutor. Until the nineteenth century we have little from

114

the converts themselves, and what they have written is often couched so much in the conventional terms learned from their Christian friends that it conveys little of the reality of their experience. As regards India, however, we are fortunate in that we possess an extensive literature, written by non-Christians who had become acquainted with the gospel and aware of its claims, but had not accepted these claims in their fullness. With the help of this material it is possible to obtain entrance into a world other than our own, and to look back with critical eyes on the work of Christian propaganda in India.

TWO EXTREME POSITIONS

At the end of the eighteenth century, when Christian work in India was resumed on a massive scale and with all the help accorded by Western prestige and power, the ancient religions of the country were in an enfeebled state. Hinduism, which over many centuries had continued to produce religious literature of great value, appeared to have lost its impetus; there was little creative thinking, and the great reforming movements seemed to have come to an end. Islam, likewise, had entered into a period of conventional acceptance rather than of challenging demand. There was vitality in some of the smaller sects, but they exercised no widespread influence on the country as a whole. All the greater was the shock when adherents of these religions became aware of this new and vigorous propaganda, which, if permitted to succeed, would produce not a reform but a revolution in the religious life of India.

The response of the great majority was simply a firm and uncompromising "No." Feeling themselves threatened, non-Christians retreated into the shell of their inherited traditions and refused to listen to or to discuss the new possibilities of faith that were being offered to them. The same attitude has been maintained by the majority over a century and a half. The great difficulty of missionary work among high-caste Hindus and Muslims today is simply that of making contact. The comparatively small number who learn English cannot be totally insulated from the gospel, since English literature and history alike are saturated with elements of the Christian tradition. The good villager, who knows only his own language, and who may in addition be illiterate since less than half of the adults of both sexes in India and Pakistan are literate even today, has little difficulty in shielding himself against the entry of new ideas. Where there is no willingness to listen, there can be no possibility of contact on the religious level.

At the other extreme, there has been great openness and readiness to consider the new ideas. When Duff started his work in Calcutta, many educated young Hindus were deeply discontented with their own religion as they knew it, evinced much admiration for Western ideas, and showed readiness at least to listen to the precepts of the Western religion. Sometimes this openness took bizarre forms, as when a group of young Hindus in Calcutta deliberately ate beef, thus breaking one of the cardinal taboos of Hinduism, in order to show that they were with it in the modern world — an experiment, incidentally, which was repeated by Mahātmā Gāndhi during his days as a student in London. With some, interest was no more than idle curiosity; with others it was combined with a sincere desire for social renewal. A small minority, confronted with the demands of the gospel, were overcome by a sense of sinfulness and alienation which could be healed only by full acceptance of Christ as Savior and by total allegiance to him. These converts have always been few; their courage and steadfastness have added memorable chapters to the history of the church of Christ in the world.

Between these two extreme positions, there are a number of other possibilities. These may be classified as the movement for the renewal of the ancient religions from within with Christian help, the movement of calculated hostility and polemic based on a knowledge of the Christian Scriptures, and the claim for peaceful coexistence and mutual recognition of the diverse religions as independent and complementary realities.

THE MOVEMENT FOR INNER RENEWAL

At this point we encounter one of the most remarkable men in the entire history of India. Rājā Rāmmohun Roy was born in 1774 of a prominent Brahman family in the district of Murshidabad in Bengal. In addition to receiving the training in Sanskrit and Hindu lore which was the normal lot of a Brahman boy, he was sent to Patna to study Arabic and Persian, and was there brought into contact with the monotheistic doctrine of Islam. Later in life he acquired Hebrew in order to read the Old Testament for himself, and even made a beginning with the study of Greek. His alert and critical intelligence was soon directed towards the problems of religion, and at the age of sixteen he wrote a remarkable pamphlet against the absurdities of idolatry. He became convinced that wisdom in its highest form is to be found in the Upanisads, and that everything in Hinduism which diverges from this high and austere standard is to be rejected as superstition and deformation.

About the year 1800 Roy took up seriously the study of English, and for a period of ten years was in the service of representatives of the East India Company. He was thus brought for the first time into contact with the Christian gospel and challenged to study the New Testament deeply. He gradually became convinced that Hinduism must remain Hinduism, but that an injection of Christian principles could bring about that renewal and purification of the ancestral faith which was his dearest object. In 1820 this Hindu published a book under the astonishing title *The Precepts of Jesus the Guide to Peace and Happiness.*[1] Explaining his purpose in the writing of the book, he affirmed that

> this simple code of religion and morality is so admirably calculated to elevate men's ideas to high and liberal notions of one God ... and is so well fitted to regulate the conduct of the human race in the discharge of their various duties

---

[1] The English works of Rāmmohun Roy were published in Calcutta (J. C. Ghosh, ed., 2 vols.) in 1887.

to God, to themselves and to society, that I cannot but hope the best effects from its promulgation in its present form.

In a later work he restated the same position:

The consequences of my long and uninterrupted researches into religious truth has been that I have found the doctrines of Christ more conducive to moral principles, and better adapted for the use of rational beings, than any other which have come to my knowledge.

It is clear that the main element in Roy's appreciation of the gospel was on the ethical side. He did not concern himself much with Christian doctrine, and was led to take up what may be generally styled a Unitarian position. It was, in fact, among Unitarians that he found the greatest sympathy and understanding.

Most unfortunately Roy became engaged in controversy with the missionaries at Serampore. Dr. Marshman felt it necessary to publish *A Defence of the Deity and Atonement of Jesus Christ, in reply to Rammohun Roy of Calcutta* (Calcutta, 1822). Roy replied with three successive defenses of his position, to which Marshman added a further reply. Others on both sides were drawn into the controversy. As is so often the case in such disputes, both sides had good reason for claiming that they were in the right. The missionaries saw clearly that the ethical teaching of Jesus cannot be separated from the totality of his work; but Christian doctrine was presented in their replies in such arid and scholastic forms that Roy had no difficulty in pointing out the weaknesses in the missionaries' case. It is sad that this first brilliant attempt by a Hindu to wrestle with the New Testament revelation did not meet with greater sympathy. On the other hand, it is gratifying to note that Roy never lost his respect for his missionary opponents and their work; when Duff opened his famous school, on the first day Roy stood beside him and encouraged the Hindu boys not to be afraid of reading the Christian *Shāstra,* from which he himself had derived so much benefit.

With Roy theory and practice went hand in hand. In 1830 he decided that a place of worship must be provided for the expression of his own views as to the nature of monotheistic faith. He had already organized the Brahmiya-Samāj, for the worship of the one eternal God, the promotion of piety, morality and charity, and the strengthening of the bonds of union between men of áll religious persuasions and creeds.[2] A building for the Hindu Theistic Church, as it was called, was opened in Calcutta on January 23, 1830. The service was divided into four parts — recitation of Vedic texts; reading from the Upanisads; delivery of a sermon in Bengali; and the singing of hymns, many of them composed by Rāmmohun Roy himself. All this was revolutionary in the Hindu world, where corporate worship and regular instruction in religious truth were unknown.

Later in the same year Roy left for his first visit to England. He never returned to India. The English climate proved too much for him and he died at Bristol on September 27, 1833. Roy had never become a Christian, retaining to the end the sacred thread of the Brahman; but he had set in motion a current of thought which still continues among educated Hindus to this day.

After Roy's death the leadership of the movement passed into the hands of Debendranāth Tagore, scion of a wealthy Brahman family, whose son Rabindranāth attained even greater fame as a poet in both Bengali and English and as winner of the Nobel Prize for literature. Debendranāth, a man of the highest integrity and intelligence, was conservative by temperament and training, and desired to follow his predecessor in making as few changes as possible in Hindu usage, leavening Hinduism from within by the recovery of older truths and by the gradual infiltration of Western ideas. The worship of the Samāj was restrained and sober, and, it must be admitted, a little cold. But the new movement was clearly meeting a need, and by 1847 no less than 767 Brahmans had accepted the Brahmo Covenant.

There was, however, a fatal weakness in the Brahmo system. Where was the seat of authority? Most of the members

---

[2] The terms of the trust deed are quoted in J. N. Farquhar, *Modern Religious Movements in India,* p. 35.

had accepted implicitly the doctrine of the verbal inspiration of the Veda, at a time in which precise knowledge of the texts of these ancient writings was very far from being widely diffused. In 1850 it was felt that accurate inquiry was needed; the report made by four young Brahmans commissioned for this purpose was highly unfavorable; both Veda and Upanisads contained many errors, and neither could be accepted as infallible. The great Indologist Max Müller in Oxford lavished almost fulsome praise on the Samāj for its courage in casting down with its own hands the wall of its fortress, and opening the door to every messenger of the truth. But, in point of fact, from that time on the Samāj rested on the shaky foundation that truth is to be accepted as the coincidence of external nature and internal intuition, an uneasy equilibrium between sheer reason on the one hand and blind faith on the other. Clearly this opened the way to individualism, "enthusiasm," and eccentricity, aspects of the Bengali character which were to be manifest in the next great Indian reformer.

Keshub Chunder Sen, who was born in 1838, was not a Brahman but a Vaidya. Brought up in an atmosphere of intense Hindu devotion, not to say superstition, Keshub received an English education at the secular Presidency College, Calcutta, and here naturally all his inherited religious notions were swept to the winds. According to his own account, he passed through a period of great distress, with a deep feeling of emptiness and worthlessness; from this he was delivered through prayer, and through a profound experience of direct access to God by which his whole future life was determined. In 1858 he stumbled on the Brahmo Samāj, and felt that he had found his home.

But Keshub was a fiery character, very little inclined to put up with what seemed to him the excessive caution of Debendranāth. He wished to push forward far more rapidly with projects of reform, such as the gradual abandonment of caste, and the rejection of superstitious ceremonies at marriage and at other crucial points of human life. Cooperation between two such different forces could not last forever. In 1868

Keshub separated himself from his friends and established his own new Samāj.

In the creed of this new body it was explicitly affirmed that "God never himself becomes man by putting on a human body. His divinity dwells in every man, and is displayed more vividly in some. Moses, Jesus Christ, Muhammad, Nānak, Caitanya, and other great teachers, appeared at special times, and conferred vast benefits on the world. They are entitled to universal gratitude and love." In spite of this limitation, Keshub evinced at all times a profound devotion to Jesus Christ. Like so many Bengalis he was a natural master of eloquence on a very high level; but, when he spoke of Jesus Christ, his spirit took wings and reached almost to the level of ecstasy. In the year 1880 he addressed to his fellow countrymen a famous challenge:

> Gentlemen, you cannot deny that your hearts have been touched, conquered and subjugated by a superior power. That power, need I tell you? is Christ. It is Christ who rules British India, and not the British government. . . . None but Jesus, none but Jesus, none but Jesus, ever deserved this bright, this precious diadem, India, and Jesus shall have it.

Why did a man who could write such things of Jesus Christ never take the ultimate step and become a Christian? The answer is clear from Keshub's own writings. The Christ presented to India by the missionaries, he held, is a purely Western and distorted Christ, and with such a Christ India will have nothing to do. Christ himself was an Asian, and so were his disciples; Christianity is a purely Oriental religion, with which the Asian feels himself immediately at home. The nature of Western man, rough, activist and imperialistic, is the most deeply inaccessible to the gospel. Hinduism needs Christ as the principle of its inner renewal; Christ needs Hinduism as the sphere in which his gospel can fully expand and manifest its own deepest reality.[3]

As he grew older Keshub grew ever more willful and

---

[3] This is well set out, with reference to the original authorities, by O. Wolff, *Christus unter den Hindus,* pp. 62-67: "Christus der Asiat."

autocratic; the result was further divisions and dissensions in the Samāj which he directed. At the time of his death his influence was perhaps less than at any time in the preceding thirty years. But he has left behind ideas, such as that of the Asiatic Christ and of the natural uncongeniality of the gospel to the Western mind, which have become almost a canonical part of modern Hinduism.

Keshub was sharply attacked by a number of missionaries, who feared the subtly corrupting influence of his eloquence, and still more sharply by his fellow countryman Nehemiah Goreh, the Brahman convert who had become a high church Anglican. Who is this Asian Christ to whom Keshub is prepared to pay such unbounded reverence? Is it the Christ of the Gospels, or is it a Christ of his own imagination? All our understanding of Christ must be constantly and strictly tested by the witness of the Gospels themselves. It is at this point that Keshub seems to have failed. He had understood, as Rāmmohun Roy did not, the problem of guilt and of reconciliation with God. He did not understand at all the part played in Christian theology by the resurrection of Jesus Christ from the dead, and the nature of the fellowship which the Christian believes himself to have with that risen Christ.

OPEN OPPOSITION

Better an open enemy than a crafty friend! When we turn from the cultured world of Rāmmohun Roy and Keshub Chunder Sen to the embittered polemics of Dayānand Sarasvati, we breathe an entirely different air.

Dayānand was born in 1824, the son of a wealthy Brahman family in Kathiawar in western India. At the end of his period of three years' study of religion, his *Guru* (teacher) laid upon him the task of reforming the Aryan (Hindu) world. To this task he devoted himself for the rest of his life. Extremely conservative in outlook, he developed an intense reverence for the Veda, and believed that salvation would come to India by the rejection of all later Hindu practices, such as idolatry, and a return to the simplicity of the Veda itself. National pride led him to affirm that the Veda is the source of all knowledge. Until India began to introduce knowledge into the West, so he believed, Egypt, Greece and Europe were sunk in total ignorance; if God had not revealed the Veda, there would be no educated men today. It need hardly be said that Dayānand was highly selective in his understanding of the Veda; Hindus, no less than Christians, can work out a highly idiosyncratic version of their own religion. But the appeal to national pride and dignity was highly effective, and in time the reformer came to have a considerable following.

Much of Dayānand's life was spent in controversy. He was a harsh and unmerciful critic of the Hindus, as he had come to know them. But the special vials of his wrath were reserved for Christianity and the Christians. In 1875 he formed the reforming society, the Ārya Samāj, which was to carry on his work. In the previous year he had published in Hindi his main work, *Satyārth Prakāsh*, "The Light of Truth" (available also in English and German). Most Indians, however critical of missionaries and Indian Christians, have spoken with the utmost respect of Jesus Christ. Not so Dayānand; no insult is too bitter, no contempt too fierce, to be heaped on the head of the founder of the Christian religion. Dayānand had made no deep study of the Bible, and had no clue as to the scientific interpretation of sacred texts. Everything is taken literally, and everything is found absurd. In his eschatological discourse Jesus is reported as having said that the stars shall fall from heaven. What could be more ridiculous? Could Jesus not have found anyone to tell him that stars do not fall? We see that he was only a carpenter, whose business in life was sawing logs and planing beams. His words found attention and acceptance only because his country was so deeply sunk in barbarism. In a cultivated country like India his teaching would have been met only with the contempt that it deserves. And so on through page after page. Destructive criticism of this kind was set forth in simple form in pamphlets in a variety of languages, and widely distributed among the people.

Dayānand's wrath was particularly directed against the

Christian doctrine of the forgiveness of sins, which he dismissed as a trick of Jesus to gain a hearing. One man's sins could not be passed on to another; the sinner suffered only for himself. If God could forgive sins, he would be unrighteous. The righteous do not need a Mediator such as Christ; the sinner cannot have a Mediator, since there is none who can forgive sins. It cannot be denied that this is so in the world of Hinduism, which knows only the iron law of retribution *(Karma)*; it is for this reason, perhaps, that one so rarely finds the word "forgiveness" even in the writings of the most modern Hindus. Nearly a century after the publication of Dayānand's best-known work, echoes of his views are still to be heard on the lower levels of Hindu controversy.

Since Dayānand took so low a view of Christianity, it could be for him nothing less than a catastrophe that any Hindu should fall into the Christian pit. Those who have so fallen must, if possible, be recovered. For the most part the Christians are the most ignorant among the people; with just a little clear Hindu instruction, it should be possible to win them back. If they are untouchables, they must be brought back to a Hinduism from which untouchability has been banished. This being the case, it is natural that some of the main activities of the Ārya Samāj have been campaigns for the reconversion of Hindus who have fallen away, campaigns which have been attended by a considerable measure of success where Christian conversion has been no more than skin-deep. The Ārya Samāj stands as a constant warning to the Christian enterprise to be watchful as to the methods that it employs, and not to be too sanguine in reckoning up the successes that it has gained.

PEACEFUL COEXISTENCE

The scene changes once again to Bengal, where in 1880 a seventeen-year-old student Narendra Nāth paid a visit to the sage Rāmakrishna Paramahamsa, to put to him questions concerning the reality of God. It is reported that Rāmakrishna had spent some time in following the rites and practices of the various religions in turn, and had found that each led to the same experience of the reality and vision of God. He therefore concluded that all religions are essentially the same. Narendra Nāth was deeply impressed by this visit, but did not adopt exactly the same view as the master. He maintained that all religions are different from one another — as different as the manifold foods that suit men of very different capacities of digestion. In all religions there is a real possibility of finding God. In all religions there are imperfections and inadequacies, but the way to progress must be not by borrowing, much less by conversion, but by inner cleansing and development of each religious system. "Each of us must sweep before his own front door." It is clear that one who holds such views must be bitterly opposed to any claim to finality or exclusiveness made on behalf of any religion. A strong anti-Christian bias is evident in the mind and writings of the young man who came to call himself in religion Swāmi Vivekānanda.

Vivekānanda's opportunity to put his ideas before the world came on the largest scale with the World's Parliament of Religions, held in Chicago in 1893. The young Bengali, with his perfect mastery of the English language and his guileless manner, quickly became one of the leading figures of the conference. On September 19 he rose to give his paper on Hinduism. Towards the close, in a calculated protest against the Christian doctrine of sin and redemption, he apostrophized the great assembly as "heirs of Immortal Bliss."

> Yea, the Hindu refuses to call you sinners. Ye are the children of God, the sharers of immortal bliss, holy and perfect beings. Ye divinities on earth — sinners? It is a sin to call a man so; it is a standing libel on human nature. Come up, O lions, and shake off the delusion that you are sheep; you are souls immortal, spirits free, blest and eternal; ye are not matter, ye are not bodies; matter is your servant, not you the servants of matter.

Such teaching chimed admirably with the liberal and humanist atmosphere of the America of those days. No less agreeable was the Swāmi's picture of a universal religion, in which all contention would cease, and all could live together peacefully.

> It was reserved for America to proclaim to all quarters of the globe that the Lord is in every religion. May He who is the Brahma of the Hindus, the Ahura-Mazda of the Zoroastrians, the Buddha of the Buddhists, the Jehovah of the Jews, the Father in Heaven of the Christians, give strength to you to carry out your noble idea.

The aim of Swāmi Vivekānanda is fairly clear. He had at first been overwhelmed by the wealth and splendor of America, and had looked around for a weapon with which to counteract or diminish this impression. He hit upon the myth of the spiritual East and the material West. This view can be maintained only by a highly selective treatment of the history of both sections of the world, but it is sufficiently plausible to have become widely current. The West is a new world, brilliantly successful on the purely material plane; let it return to the ancient fountains of wisdom in the East to be refreshed and renewed. There must be no question of conversion. The Christian can perfectly practice the principles of Vedānta without ceasing to be a Christian. Let him learn to develop in his own way and in his own tradition, and let him be willing to allow the Hindu to do the same.[4] Clearly, if this view is adopted, the Christian mission in any traditional sense of the term is at an end. There may be a fellowship of exchange, but there can be no proclamation of the Lordship of Christ over all the world.

Vivekānanda died in 1902 at the age of 39. But he left behind him a band of devoted disciples, who made it their task to carry on the work of their master in the development of the Rāmakrishna Mission, which had been founded by

---

[4] His speech on September 27, 1893: "Do I wish that the Christian would become Hindu? God forbid. Do I wish that the Hindu or Buddhist would become Christian? God forbid. . . . The Christian is not to become a Hindu or a Buddhist, nor a Hindu or a Buddhist to become a Christian. But each religion must assimilate the spirit of the other and yet preserve its individuality, and grow according to its own law of growth." Quoted in D. S. Sarma, *The Renaissance of Hinduism,* p. 272.

him in 1897. This admirable body carries on educational and social work in many parts of India in a spirit of great devotion and self-sacrifice. It may be said that imitation is the sincerest form of flattery, and that the mission aims to undercut Christianity by doing better than the Christians the very things which have their inspiration in the Christian gospel and not in the Hindu scriptures. But such devotion is found only where something higher than a merely negative and polemical spirit is at work.

CONCLUSION

Some years ago a prize was offered in the University of Cambridge for an essay on "The Indirect Effect of Christian Missions in India."[5] Only one aspect of these indirect effects has been dealt with in this chapter, and only by a process of selection of what seem to be the most important movements. But what has been written is enough to show that the influence of the Christian gospel radiates out far beyond the limits of the Christian church. Conversions have been comparatively few. But the preaching of the gospel has set in motion in the non-Christian religions a process of self-questioning and self-criticism which will not be stayed. An inner transformation seems to be going forward, and the transformation is almost exclusively in the Christian direction. How far this will go it is impossible to say. This is part of the atmosphere in which Christian work is carried on in India today.

---

[5] The prize was won by Mr. R. S. Wilson, whose work was published in 1928 by James Clarke, London.

VII

THE GROWTH OF INDEPENDENCE

✦ NATIONAL STIRRINGS

BRITISH POWER IN INDIA WAS MAINTAINED WITH AN EXTRAORDI-narily small exercise or manifestation of force. There was the "steel frame" of the Indian Civil Service, with never more than a thousand fully enrolled members. There was a small professional army, for the most part guarding the northwest frontiers against the tribesmen whose appetites were constantly inflamed by the sight of the more prosperous plains and the possibility of loot. Over the greater part of the country the army was invisible. Such a state of affairs would have been impossible if the great majority of the population had not settled down with a fair measure of contentment under the new foreign government which had replaced the old foreign government of the Moguls, and brought about peace, order and possibilities of progress such as the Moguls had provided only at the height of their power.

But there were always elements of discontent. Indians were employed by the government, but only in the lower ranks of the administration. There was little scope for ambition and achievement. The British had generously provided uni-versities, but without much thought about the question as to what the graduates would do when they had finished their university course. The most intelligent among them followed the profession of law, in which great fortunes were to be made. But many failed to find any employment at all, or had to be content with inferior positions, such as that of station-masters in small stations on the railways, which they did not feel to be adequate reward for the laborious processes of study. In other parts of the world unemployment means unemployment in the so-called working class; in India it has meant unemployment of the educated minority. In these circles economic and social distress could very easily be transformed into political disquiet and into the conviction that nothing would go right in India until the foreigner had been driven out.

The influence of Europeans at this stage of development was far from being altogether helpful. The majority of them could get along extremely well with the natural aristocracy of India, the princes and the great landholders; equally well with the peasants whose sterling qualities they were ready to recognize. Relations were much more difficult with the *Babu,* the educated or half-educated man, not quite at home in his own Indian world, the customs of which he had largely discarded, and not at all at home in the Western world which he had come to know through books but with the social usages of which he was almost wholly unfamiliar. His very uncertainty often made him gauche, unduly sensitive and arrogant. The undisguised contempt often shown by Europeans for the members of this rising class was one of the main causes of the intense anti-British feeling that has manifested itself from time to time even to the present day. Who will dare to smile, unless with respect and even affection, at the true story of the two Brahman gentlemen, eager students of Shakespeare, who one day decided to do something really English, bought a pot of strawberry jam, and ate it with their fingers?

To wise observers it became clear that British rule in India could not go on forever as it had been. Changes must take place, and always in the direction of greater independence and self-rule. The first steps in this direction were, however, marked by an almost unbelievable caution and sobriety. The Indian National Congress held its first meeting in 1885, but it spent a large part of its time in extolling the benefits that had been brought to India by British rule! It was not long, however, before the language of Indian patriots became more forceful and less complimentary. By the end of the first world war, during which the whole British Empire had admired the courage and resolution of the Indian troops who had stood side by side with British troops in some of the most desperate encounters of the war, it was clear that India was about to demand a great deal more than had as yet been granted, and that British liberal sentiment was prepared to go a very long way to grant what India desired. In 1919 the Montague-Chelmsford reforms were set in motion, to give Indians a far greater share than before in constitutional responsibility for the affairs of their own country. It was officially declared that the aim of the British government was "the progressive realization of responsible government in India as an integral part of the British Empire." In a notable proclamation King George V stated that "I have watched with understanding and sympathy the growing desire of my Indian people for representative institutions. . . . With the same sympathy and with redoubled interest I shall watch the progress along this road. . . . I pray to Almighty God that by his wisdom and under his guidance India may be led to greater prosperity and contentment, and may grow to *the fulness of political freedom.*"

During the next thirty years there was never any basic difference of purpose between responsible leaders in Britain and responsible leaders of the Indian national movement. Everything seemed set for peaceful progress in the direction desired by all. Two factors — a tragic event, and the personality of one man — rendered this peaceful progress impossible.

After the end of the war there had been much disturbance in India, one of the hottest centers of disaffection being Amritsar in the Punjab. On April 13, 1919, General Dyer, in charge of the Indian troops in that city, ordered a large crowd to disperse, and when they failed to do so, gave the order to fire. General Dyer seems to have been unaware that the crowd could not disperse, since he was blocking with his troops the only exit from the Jallianwala Bagh; firing continued for ten minutes, and more than three hundred people were killed. The threatened rebellion at once collapsed; but the harm done to the British name in India was almost irreparable.

One of the consequences of Amritsar was that a lawyer, recently returned to India from South Africa, Mohandas Karamchand Gāndhi, decided that it was no longer possible to cooperate with the British. India's freedom was to be won by non-cooperation. Every offer made by the British government, however generous, was to be rejected. Indians were to be persuaded that they could win their freedom by the new weapons of non-violence, *Ahimsā,* and peaceful civil disobedience. This is not the place to record in detail the successive attempts made by the British government to reach agreement with the nationalists, and the successive waves of civil disobedience by which those well-meant efforts were frustrated. The time has as yet hardly come at which an entirely impartial account of these events can be written.

Mahātmā Gāndhi's influence on the Christian cause in India was ambivalent. On the one hand, he made no secret of the fact that he had been profoundly influenced by the New Testament and the person of Jesus Christ. He encouraged young Hindus to read the Gospels, and there is no doubt that thousands of them did so under his influence. This opened the way to new evangelistic methods. Over many years the eloquent American preacher Stanley Jones, who was a close personal friend of the Mahātmā, traveled round all the great cities of India, gathering audiences of educated Hindus and Muslims, who would listen spell-bound to the presentation of the Christian message. On the other hand, Gāndhi affirmed that he was and always would be a Hindu. In 1925 he delivered a celebrated address to missionaries in Calcutta, in which he told them that he found in the Indian classic the Bhagavad Gītā deeper truths even than those which he found in the Gospels.[1] He assured his Hindu friends that they could find in Hinduism all that they needed, incorporating into their Hindu faith anything that they found to be of value in the Christian gospel, and that to leave the faith in which you have been born for another is disobedience to the will of God and is bound to bring about disorder. The effect of this teaching was that many inquirers, who might otherwise have become Christians, decided to stay within the Hindu fold.

Missionaries in India differed considerably in their attitudes to these new movements. Almost without exception the attitude not only of British missionaries but of those of other nations also was conservative. They greatly valued the peace and order brought by the British rāj, the uninterrupted tranquility in which they could carry on their work, and the help accorded at many points by the government. They feared disorder and disturbance. Some, however, were of a different mind, notable among them the Anglican Charles Freer Andrews, who became an intimate friend of Gāndhi, Tagore and other Indian leaders, and proclaimed himself uncompromisingly in favor of Indian freedom. But, even among the missionaries who took a progressive view, there was disagreement as to the methods and the parties that were to be supported. Since the Congress party under Mr. Gāndhi and Mr. Nehru won out, it has been natural for a later generation to identify the Indian national movement with this single stream. But in fact there were many others. A number of missionaries felt themselves more attracted by the Indian liberals, men who had drunk deeply at the founts of the English liberal traditions, and were prepared to move slowly in the direction of a genuine democracy; some of them like Sir Mirza Ismail, for many years Prime Minister of the state of Mysore, had acquired wide administrative experience.

Indian Christians tended still to be little interested in politics. They belonged for the most part to the communities which had been trained over many centuries to think that

---

[1] The relevant passage is quoted in W. D. P. Hill, *The Bhagavad Gītā*, p. viii.

their first duty was to obey; they were accustomed to managing, often with considerable efficiency, their local affairs, but did not look far beyond their village borders. A great change came about in the late 1920's. By that time it had become clear that the star of Mr. Gāndhi was in the ascendency. The great capitalists of India, wanting to safeguard their own future in an independent India, began to cast in their lot with him. Gāndhi needed large sums of money for his anti-British campaigns. An alliance was struck between nationalists and capitalists, which was to be of great importance in future political developments. Just at the same time a number of leading Indian Christians, among whom Mr. K. T. Paul, a South Indian layman who had rendered notable service in the Y.M.C.A., and was one of the first secretaries of the National Christian Council of India, may be specially mentioned, took up eagerly the Indian national cause, and threw in their lot with the Congress party.[2]

INDIA A NATION

The second world war introduced new perils into the situation. In 1942 the Congress was successful in spreading disorder far and wide in India, and for a moment it seemed possible that the Japanese who were massed on the northeastern frontier would be able to occupy large parts of India. This did not come about, and gradually the Japanese peril receded. But at the same time an inner danger was growing. Mr. Gāndhi always claimed that the Congress was a national party, in which all Indians could find their place without distinction of class or religion. A number of eminent Muslims were in fact among his lieutenants. But from 1940 on it became increasingly clear that the majority of Muslims were dissatisfied with the Congress program, and would not settle down happily in an independent India under the domination of the Congress. Under the lead of Mohammed Ali Jinnah

---

[2] The life of Mr. K. T. Paul has been written by H. A. Popley, *K. T. Paul: Christian Leader*. Mr. Paul had been a nationalist for many years before he took an open stand as a Christian political leader.

they began to demand the independent Muslim state of Pakistan.

Some believe that, if Nehru and Gāndhi had been willing to make certain concessions, the disaster of separation might have been avoided. In view of the rigid attitude of the Muslims, this must be regarded as quite uncertain. In any case the two Congress leaders were so convinced that the unity of Mother India could not possibly be broken up that they refused all the concessions that might have pacified the Muslims. So when in 1947 Clement Attlee, Socialist Prime Minister of Great Britain, decided that the time had come at which India's independence must be brought about and sent Lord Mountbatten out to settle the matter once for all, India did indeed become independent, but a terrible price had to be paid for that independence. Tensions between the races and religions had been steadily mounting; suddenly the explosion took place. Within a few weeks, at the lowest computation, three quarters of a million people lost their lives in a series of insane and horrifying massacres. Mutual trust was lost to such an extent that well-intentioned Hindus could not help Muslims and well-meaning Muslims could not help Hindus. Mercifully, the fury wore itself out, as it usually does, within a few weeks and calm was restored. But many years must pass before the memory of those terrible weeks can be effaced.

When the terror was over, it was clear that the greatest gift that the British had given to the Indian subcontinent, a political unity coextensive with the geographical unity, had gone forever. If this book had been written twenty-two years ago, it would have been called *The Story of the Christian Church in India;* now, to make clear what it is that we are talking about, we have to add the words *and Pakistan.*

THE EMERGENCE OF INDIAN CHRISTIAN LEADERSHIP

All wise missionaries had seen that the building up of an Indian church must be the work not of foreign missionaries, but of Indian leaders. Talks on this subject began a long time ago. Correspondence, more than a century old, in the possession of the writer, shows that at that time dis- cussions were already being held as to the possibility of the appointment of an Indian bishop. The missionaries of the day were by no means adverse to the idea, but the letters show clearly the point to which they had advanced. The basic principle was that a man is responsible to the authority that pays him. Therefore, pastors or catechists paid by the mission could not come under the control of an Indian bishop; he could be the head only of that part of the work of the church for the financial maintenance of which he could make himself responsible. The idea of a truly Indian church, in which the missionary would take his place alongside his Indian colleagues on a basis of equality, had not yet risen above the horizon.

One of the problems in the development of Indian leader- ship was the simple fact that very few Indian Christians were as well educated as their Western friends. It was a great step forward when a group of missionary societies decided to put an end to this inequality by seeing to it that the pos- sibility was provided in India of a theological education as good as that which the majority of missionaries had re- ceived. In 1910 the United Theological College came into existence at Bangalore,[3] with as its first principal the Dane Dr. L. P. Larsen, the most distinguished missionary of his time in South India. In 1917, as we have seen, Serampore was reconstituted. After consultation with the government of Bengal, which made no objection, it was decided to offer the degrees of Bachelor of Divinity and Licentiate in Theol- ogy. Following the affiliating pattern, to which we have re- ferred in connection with the founding of universities in India, Serampore was prepared to offer its degrees to students in other institutions, and even in certain circumstances to students studying privately. It was intended that the Seram- pore B.D. should be on the same level as similar examina-

---

[3] By a pleasing coincidence I am revising these pages in the library of this College, which I first visited in 1926 in the company of Dr. E. Stanley Jones.

tions held by Western universities. If the intention was not always carried into effect, that must be laid more to the charge of the general level of Indian education than to any failure on the part of Serampore. At about the same time Bishop's College, Calcutta, the great foundation of the first bishop of Calcutta, which had sunk to being little more than a hostel for university students, was restored to its original function as the chief training center for Anglican students of theology. The Methodists later made their contribution by founding Leonard College, Jubbulpore; and a little later still the Lutherans added their institution at Rajamundry in the Telugu area of South India. India thus had five colleges in which the study of theology was seriously pursued under teachers some of whom could have adorned any theological faculty in the West.

It was not long before advantage was taken of the new situation to raise Indians to positions of leadership in the church such as they had never enjoyed before. Some non-church organizations, such as the Y.M.C.A., had been highly adventurous in promoting Indian leadership; the churches on the whole had suffered from an excess of timidity.

For some years the great bishop of Madras, Henry White-head, had been convinced that the time had come for the appointment of an Indian bishop. He found his man in Vedanayakam Samuel Azariah, son of one of the village pastors in Tinnevelly, who had made his name in the service of the Y.M.C.A. and as one of the founders of the Indian Mission-ary Society of Tinnevelly in 1903. Azariah was a man of con-siderable ability, of tireless industry in study and of un-feigned devotion, never quite sure of himself and therefore inclined to be at times aggressive and authoritarian, but nevertheless with lineaments of real greatness. He was not afraid of Europeans and could work with them. Thus he was able to leave the administration of his diocese to three ex-ceptionally able archdeacons, while he attended to his own work as teacher, inspirer and leader in the development of a great mass movement. Azariah was consecrated as the first Indian bishop of the Anglican Church at Christmastide 1912.

At first he was given only a small area; as he himself guile-lessly explained, Bishop Whitehead defended the appoint-ment on the ground that it was a small area, and not much harm would be done if he made a mess of it. As his ability manifested itself, he was entrusted with ever larger areas, until his diocese of Dornakal contained a larger number of Indian Christians than any other Anglican diocese in India. In a sense Azariah spoiled the market by his very greatness. Other Indians served with distinction as assistant bishops; but at the time of his death he still had only one Indian colleague among the diocesan bishops.

In 1923 the Roman Catholic Church finally overcame its long hesitancy. Mgr. Tiburtius Roche, a descendant of one of Xavier's flock on the Fisher Coast, was consecrated to be bishop of Tuticorin, a long narrow coastal diocese, in which almost all the Christians belonged to the Fisher caste. At the same time all European Roman Catholic priests, except for one or two engaged in education, were removed elsewhere, leaving the new bishop as head of a purely Indian church. Here again progress was slow. Gradually the South Indian sees came to be guided by Indian bishops; but it was only in the period of India's independence that the Westerners came to be outnumbered by their Indian colleagues. More-over, bishops of the Roman obedience were subject to strict supervision on the part of the Apostolic Delegate, at one time the American Mooney, later a gifted Dutchman Kierkels, who as the direct representative of the Pope took precedence over any other archbishop or bishop.

In 1930 the Methodist Church of Southern Asia took the step of appointing J. R. Chitambar as its first Indian bishop. The Lutherans had to wait still longer, their first Indian bishop having been appointed after the end of the period which we are now considering. But all the churches were on the way. Slowly and doubtfully, but in the end irresistibly, the current turned. Everywhere men saw that an Indian church could not emerge until the church was provided with Indian leaders, and that leaders would not emerge until perhaps imperfectly qualified persons were given the opportunity to exercise leadership. As chairmen of councils, as principals of colleges, as directors of hospitals, the Indians were beginning to take their place. The women were only a short distance behind the men, though naturally the range of positions which they could fill was more limited.

ORGANIZING AN INDIAN CHURCH

It is no use having leaders, unless there is something for them to lead. The early missionaries had been for the most part prepared to let their converts go on in a state of total dependence on the emissaries from the West. There was, of course, consultation with the local Christians; but the authority of the missionary was very great, and in the end all the important decisions were made by him, perhaps alone, perhaps in consultation with missionary colleagues. As early as the middle of the nineteenth century, missionary statesmen such as Rufus Anderson in America[4] and Henry Venn in Britain had seen that this state of things could not go on forever, and that the church, in order to be a church, must grow in independence and must learn to stand on its own feet. As early as 1863 some rather feeble attempts had been made to set up church councils in Anglican fields in India; but the power of decision was still kept firmly in the hands of foreigners, and progress was very slow.

At this point Tirunelveli again for a moment took the center of the stage. After the death in 1889 of the first assistant bishop for the Church Missionary Society area, Edward Sargent, who had given more than fifty years of service to India and ruled his area with a rod of iron, it was decided that much more radical steps must be taken in the direction of genuine self-government. There were now more than 54,000 Christians in the area with nearly seventy Indian clergymen. The Church Missionary Society in London sent out one of its secretaries, a very able man named John Barton,

---

4 In 1854 Rufus Anderson visited India. This visit was strategic in introducing to American missions the ideas of self-governing congregations and ordained Indian ministers, in which their British colleagues had been pioneering at a slightly earlier date.

with instructions that he was to bring into being a really
democratic and indigenous system. Barton divided the area
into fifteen "circles," for each of which a committee was to
be elected; the important thing was that each committee was
to have at its head *ex officio* an Indian clergyman, and was
gradually to take over responsibility for all local work, including the development of the self-support by which that local
work was to be maintained. But at the center was to be a
district council, and of this a missionary was always to be
chairman. On the Executive Committee four missionaries were
to have *ex officio* seats. At first the Tinnevelly Christians
tended to look to the missionary for guidance, and to take
only the action which was likely to be approved by higher
authority. It gradually dawned on the members that they
really were expected to think for themselves and to make
the decisions that seemed to them to be according to the will
of God. Always accustomed to fighting their missionaries,
the hardy Tamil Christians now discovered that it was really
more profitable to let their pugnacity exercise itself in more
constructive channels.[5]

The Tirunelveli model was adopted far and wide throughout the country, with variations from area to area and denomination to denomination. But in the last resort these
were still missionary organizations, and Indian control failed
just where it was most needed — at the center. Once again,
it was a great bishop of Tirunelveli, Harry Waller (Tirunelveli 1914-23, Madras 1923-41), who saw that the whole missionary structure must be overturned, and replaced by that
of a diocese in which the missionary would be a servant and
no longer a master. It happened that the generation of really
great missionaries who had worked the Barton scheme disappeared one after the other just before Waller came in as
bishop, so he had the opportunity to carry out his plan
unhindered. In 1925 the diocese was provided with a constitution in which the word "missionary" does not occur, except in
one single chapter dealing with the relationship between the

---

5 Mr. Barton's work is described in the article, "The Native Church in
Tinnevelly," *Church Missionary Intelligencer* (1891), pp. 586-595.

missionary in the field and the society which had sent him to India. From now on the missionary was to be placed and directed by the diocese, in every committee of which there was a strong Indian majority.

Gradually internal liberty was being won from missionary control. But the Indian churches were still at almost every point dependent on distant bodies in the West, of which they were regarded as satellites. This too was a system that must disappear. An Indian church might be aided from abroad; it must not be directed or ruled.

The Anglicans took the lead in the process of emancipation. Under the guidance of a wise bishop of Calcutta, Foss Westcott, son of the famous New Testament scholar, the Church of India, Burma, and Ceylon[6] came into being in 1930. Until that time the Anglican Church in India had been legally a part of the Church of England. Bishops of the primary sees were appointed by the Crown, others by the Archbishop of Canterbury. No single word of the English Book of Common Prayer could be altered. Bishop Cotton's beautiful prayer for India, which was widely used, had to be printed on the inside of the cover of the Prayer Book, and not in the text. Now all was changed. The Indian church could and did draw up its own constitution. It could revise its liturgy. It would elect its own bishops. While retaining the fullest communion with the see of Canterbury, it would make plain its determination to guide its own destiny as a fully self-governing church.

For the Roman Catholic Church, clearly, no such independence was possible; and moves to give the Indian episcopate greater freedom belong to a later period of Indian church history. Other churches also, because of their strictly centralized organization, were hindered in their desire for greater independence in the field. For instance, we have noted that the American Methodists had started out on the course of the Indianization of the episcopate in India, and were making rapid progress in this direction. But under the constitution of that church, all the bishops were chosen and

---

6 Since 1947 the Church of India, Pakistan, Burma and Ceylon.

appointed at the general conference held in the United States and not by any Indian body. When the World Council of Churches came into being in 1948, the Methodist Church of Southern Asia did not qualify as an autonomous church under the rules which the council had adopted for the admission of churches to membership. Similarly, British Methodist missionaries were members of a conference in London, a privilege which they were loath to lose; while many important decisions could be made in India, others were held in reserve for the central body in London. At one point in the negotiations for church union in South India, it was touch and go whether the green light would be given by the conference for further advance towards union.

Apart from such technicalities, there was one problem which weighed heavily on all developments towards the emergence of a genuinely Indian church — financial dependence on the West. The majority of Indian Christians were poor. Though progress towards self-support had been made in many regions, without financial help from the West the Indian church would have been gravely weakened and in some areas might have collapsed. Moreover, whereas the Indian Christian was prepared to give more than generously for something that he could see, such as a new church in his own village, he was little interested in central institutions such as theological seminaries, which, however indispensable, did not immediately present themselves to his consciousness. If such institutions were to be maintained, it seemed likely that Western help would be needed for a very long time. To some extent human nature demands the implementation of the old saying, "The man who pays the piper calls the tune." The desire of the missionary societies to keep a measure of control over the money sent out by them was not due just to Western arrogance. Mission funds are contributed for the most part by comparatively poor Christians in the West, often at the price of real hardship to themselves; the missionary societies have felt themselves to be in the position of trustees, responsible to see to it that the money sent out by them was really spent for the glory of God, and not to carry out the caprices of a possibly less than fully responsible Indian church body. Nevertheless, this distant control has often been found galling by Indian leaders. There may well be only one Westerner on a committee; but if he is the treasurer, his single voice may carry more weight than that of all the Indian delegates put together.

AN INDIAN CHRISTIAN SPIRIT

A church could become entirely independent in self-government and self-support, and yet remain in reality a foreign church. As we have seen, one of the criticisms made by the non-Christians was that the Indian church was really a foreign body which had no genuine place in Indian society. Could the church lose this foreignness without ceasing to be a Christian fellowship?

From an early period in Christian history in India, the Indian spirit had begun to manifest itself at certain points. Hymns and lyrics had been composed in Indian meters and set to Eastern tunes. Two notable poets had made their contribution to the development of Christian literature in India. H. A. Krishna Pillai, a high-caste convert from Hinduism, had produced in 1894 a remarkable poem of almost epic proportions named *Rakshanya Yāthrikam,* the "Pilgrimage of Salvation," which, though based on Bunyan's *Pilgrim's Progress,* had been thoroughly rethought in Indian terms, and set forth in glowing verse and imagery the devotion of a profoundly convinced Indian Christian.[7] Nārāyan Vāman Tilak, who died in 1919, was also a convert, in this case from a Brahman family in western India, who, in addition to many other writings in prose and verse, enriched the Marathi hymnbook with more than 200 hymns.[8] But, though the devotional value of such writings was very high, the theological content was hardly original.

Sooner or later a church must work out its own theology;

---

[7] See A. J. Appasāmy, *Indian Christian Poet* (World Christian Books, no. 56, London: U.S.C.L., Lutterworth Press, 1966).

[8] See L. Tilak, *From Brahma to Christ* (World Christian Books, no. 9, London: U.S.C.L., Lutterworth Press, 1956).

this is likely to stand in close relation to the great traditions of Christian thought in East and West; but this does not exclude the possibility of, indeed the need for, varieties of insight and approach. The problem in India was that in some ways the missionaries had done their work too well. Western ways of worship and Western ways of theological expression had become dear to ministers and laymen alike. Any attempt to find a more Indian expression of Christian theology was likely to be sharply criticized by the orthodox as a tendency to regress to the supposed darkness of Hinduism.

Other tendencies were at work, however, not uninfluenced by the current trend towards nationalism in the Indian church. A group of educated and able Indian laymen, of whom the best known were V. Chakkarai and P. Chenchiah,[9] both men of the highest ability, were strongly opposed to missionary dominance and the overpowering influence of the West, and eager to see the Indian Christian spirit set free to draw more fully on the great traditions of Indian thought and philosophy. In 1938 this group produced a book with the title *Re-thinking Christianity in India*. In part this was intended as an answer to the theology of Hendrik Kraemer, who in his famous book *The Christian Message in a non-Christian World*, written in preparation for the Tambaram Conference of that same year, had rather cavalierly swept aside all the non-Christian religions as evidence of man's rebellion against God. This theology was naturally most uncongenial to the Indian national spirit. Proposals were not infrequently heard at this time that the reading of the Old Testament, as a purely Jewish book, should be abandoned in Christian worship, and should be replaced by selected readings from the ancient Hindu classics. Such unhistorical thinking was characteristic of that stage of the independence movement. It cannot be said that the Chakkarai-Chenchiah group was very successful in giving genuinely Indian content

9 An article on "Chenchiah's Christology" by S. Wesley Ariarajah appeared in the *Bangalore Theological Forum* (no. 1, 1968), pp. 46-61, and a much fuller study is: D. A. Thangasamy, *The Theology of Chenchiah* (Bangalore: CISRS, 1967).

to Christian theology. Not much is gained by substituting Sanskrit terms for the familiar terms of Greek origin, unless a much deeper process of re-thinking has taken place. Perhaps the psychological situation favorable to such re-thinking could not be reached until the political independence of India had been achieved.

In this same period voices were heard uplifted in favor of a change in missionary methods — simplicity, as against the cumbersome machinery of European ways. The most famous of all Indian Christians, Sādhu Sundar Singh, by his wandering life of extreme simplicity and by the direct appeal of his devotional writings, had convinced many for the first time that India had something new to contribute to the knowledge of Christ. Interest in the work of the Sādhu continued long after his disappearance in 1929.

The āshram, a settlement of people devoted to simplicity of life and fellowship in service, had played a great part in Indian life. Could not the same method be adapted to Christian purposes? This question was asked by K. T. Paul as early as 1912. In the generation following a large number of Christian āshrams came into being. Two may be mentioned by way of illustration. In 1921 the Christukula Āshram was founded in the Tamil country by two doctors, Jesudason, a member of a prominent Christian family, and Forrester-Paton, a Scot; the aim of this institution was to combine medical and evangelistic work on a genuinely Indian basis. The Christa Seva Sangh at Poona (also in 1921, but later divided by the formation of the Christa Prema Seva Sangh in 1934) arose out of the work of an Anglican missionary, the Rev. J. C. Winslow. Its aim was to create a Christian atmosphere in which the educated Hindu would yet feel himself at home. The central problem of these āshrams has been that in most cases they have come into existence through the devotion of one or two Christians of strong character and clear convictions; it has proved hard for others to enter into such a closed fellowship, and, though the āshrams have continued to exist, they have not expanded in the way that a number of Roman Catholic orders have grown from small beginnings to great achievements.

At one point the Indian Christian situation is paradoxical. The early missionaries of all confessions built churches much like those to which they were accustomed in the West, regardless of the exigencies of the Indian climate. To this type of architecture Indian Christians have become much attached. In consequence, attempts to use Hindu architectural patterns for a place of Christian worship, as in the elaborate church at the Christukula *Āshram,* have proved by no means popular with the local Christians. Their view is that, just as a Hindu temple looks like a temple, and a mosque looks like a mosque, so also a church should look like a church. There is more in this argument than perhaps meets the eye. A Hindu temple is a place where a god dwells. Ceremonies are regularly carried out, but there is no provision for congregational worship. A mosque is a place where *men only* meet for worship. There is something in Christian congregational worship which is not to be found in any other religion. Obviously it is undesirable that the church should remain wedded to a purely Western tradition; but nothing is gained by mere borrowing; the outward expression of Indian Christianity must develop spontaneously out of a deeper apprehension of its inner truth.

STRIVINGS AFTER UNITY

The unity of the Indian subcontinent was the greatest achievement of the British in India, and the great gift which for a century was conferred by British rule. It was lamentable that the Christian forces, pledged to the unity of all mankind in Christ, should come in as a force making for division. It could not be otherwise in the divided state of the Christian world; but it is not surprising that from an early date Christians should have been uncomfortable about their divisions.

Relations between Roman Catholics and Protestants remained poor until the end of the period with which we are dealing. Quite early in the nineteenth century signs of Protestant unity began to appear.

In many fields cooperation was found to be possible. Notable among these fields was cooperative work on the translation of the Bible. At the least, it is highly inconvenient that more than one version of the Scriptures should be circulating in a single language area. Perfect success was not always achieved. The union version of the Tamil Bible which appeared in 1869 was not wholly successful in replacing the older Lutheran version completed by Philip Fabricius at the end of the eighteenth century. In the Santal region also two forms of the Bible were in use, the stumbling-block here being that ancient problem of Bible translators, the choice of a term for the word "God" in a language without Christian traditions.

From 1855 onwards missionaries began to meet regularly in conference. The Bangalore Conference of 1879, which gathered a large number of missionaries and a smaller number of Indian Christians from all over South India, was notable not least for the fact that the nature and emergence of an Indian Christian church was a subject of serious discussion. The Madras Conference of 1900 carried development a stage further in that those who came were delegates of societies or churches and not simply interested persons, and that careful attention had been given to preparation and to the choice of themes.

Such conferences, however, met *ad hoc;* as soon as they were at an end, the organization was dissolved and there was no particular reason to suppose that a similar conference would ever again be held. The great revolution came with the first World Missionary Conference held at Edinburgh in 1910, and the development for the first time in the non-Roman world of permanent organs to serve the cause of continuous cooperation in Christian service. In the years after 1910 Dr. John R. Mott made a great journey through Asia, in the course of which he was successful in bringing into existence national Christian bodies in a number of countries. The National Missionary Conference was organized in 1912.

It was reconstituted in 1922 as the National Christian Council of India. The change in name indicated a real change in character; from this point on it was laid down that at least half the members of the conference must be Indian nationals. One who served on both councils[10] has left on record his opinion that, though man for man the earlier council was the abler, the second was far more satisfactory in that for the first time the genuine voice of the Indian church began to be heard. These councils were made up of a mixed bag of churches, missions and other bodies such as the Bible Society. They had no coercive power at all; their effectiveness was to depend entirely on the wisdom of their deliberations and decisions. But within a short time, together with the regional councils which grew up around them, they came to play an indispensable role as a forum for the discussion of common problems and interests. An admirably conducted periodical, *The National Christian Council Review,* is an indispensable source of accurate information on all aspects of Indian church history since the date of the foundation of the council.

PEACEFUL COEXISTENCE

If five or six different missions are working in one place, any non-Christian who wishes to become a Christian is faced with a cruel dilemma: to which of the Christian bodies should he give his allegiance? To avert such problems as far as possible, the missions at an early date began to adopt the so-called principle of comity, or peaceful coexistence. This was one of the main subjects of discussion at the large international conference held in London in 1888; the problem was one with which many countries other than India were also concerned. The basic principle of comity is that, where one Protestant mission is at work, another should not enter in without good reason, and that converts of one mission should not be accepted into membership by another without discussion between both the churches concerned. At the

10 The Rev. W. E. S. Holland of the Church Missionary Society, personally communicated to the writer.

Madras Decennial Conference of 1902 an arbitration board was set up to deal with all such problems. This method certainly solved many problems, and prevented a great deal of harmful rivalry. But at several important points it failed to meet the needs of the churches.

In the first place, families came to be divided by religious as well as by geographical factors. Some of the great Christian families which had spread throughout the whole of the Tamil area found themselves by the accident of geography divided up among half a dozen Christian confessions, some of which did not permit intercommunion with those of other forms of the Christian faith. An outstanding leader of the Congregationalist Church, C. J. Lucas, has left it on record that his father was a Lutheran, his mother a Congregationalist, his wife an Anglican, one son in the South India United Church, another confirmed by an Anglican bishop, one brother-in-law a Methodist, and several other relatives Roman Catholics.

Secondly, ecclesiastical boundaries tended to follow those of government units; thus, where the boundary was a small stream, converts in two adjoining villages, belonging to the same caste and closely related to one another, might find themselves as Christians launched into entirely separate confessions.

Thirdly, there was the problem of the wandering Indian Christian. In seasons when the rains failed, thousands of young men would go off to the tea plantations in the hills, often finding themselves in an area in which the church to which they belonged was not represented. What should they do? Should they refrain from Christian worship, or find a temporary home in whatever church might happen to be there? The Lutherans on the whole told their members that they must wait for a visit from a Lutheran pastor — and the wait might be a very long one. Other churches felt it better that their young men should become temporary members of some other church, with undiminished rights of membership in their own church on their return.[11]

---

[11] See B. G. M. Sundkler, *The Church of South India,* pp. 31-32.

Such inconveniences tended to turn the minds of church leaders more and more in the direction of corporate unity as the only finally satisfactory solution to the problem of Christian division. But the pragmatic arguments were not in the end those that prevailed. Perhaps the greatest achievement of biblical theology in the twentieth century has been the recovery of the doctrine of the church as an integral part of the gospel. In the nineteenth century individualism had been so strong that the church had come to seem almost like an optional appendix to a gospel in which it played no essential part. The new theology saw plainly that God, in principle, deals with a fellowship and not only with individuals, and that to be a Christian means to belong to a people of God, the unity of which should be evident to the non-believer and not merely a secret experience of the faithful.

TOWARDS CORPORATE UNION

To the Presbyterians belongs the honor of taking the first steps towards visible union in India. In 1901 the first South India United Church was formed by the union of three Presbyterian missions, two from Scotland and one from the United States of America. This was enlarged in the formation of the second South India United Church in 1908; to this Congregationalists as well as Presbyterians adhered, and one district in Ceylon was added to the seven in India. Observers asked themselves whether this somewhat loose union should not be regarded rather as a federation than as a church; the members of the South India United Church declared that they regarded themselves as members of a church, and would desire to determine all their planning and their actions on the basis of this understanding.

To anticipate a little the chronological sequence of our story, it may be mentioned here that the experiment in South India was reflected in North India, when in 1924 Congregationalists and Presbyterians over a very wide area joined together in the formation of the United Church of North India, completely independent from the United Church in the south but on closely similar lines.

A new impetus came from the Tranquebar conference of pastors in 1919. The Anglican church in India had not remained unaffected by the new currents in favor of union, one of the most vocal spokesmen of this point of view being Bishop Henry Whitehead. Of the thirty-three pastors assembled at Tranquebar, only two were foreigners, one American and one English. The primary theme of the conference was the evangelization of India; the question of church union arose as a corollary to this primary concern. The Tranquebar Manifesto is a historic and prophetic document, which needs to be read as a whole; here space forbids the quotation of more than the crucial sentences:

> We face together the titanic task of the winning of India for Christ — one fifth of the human race. Yet, confronted by such an overwhelming responsibility, we find ourselves rendered weak and relatively impotent by our unhappy divisions — divisions for which we were not responsible, and which have been, as it were, imposed upon us from without; divisions which we did not create and which we do not desire to perpetuate.[12]

The Manifesto was grain sown in a well-prepared field. The matter was taken up by the churches most concerned, and an invitation was sent to all churches in South India to participate in a serious quest for full, visible and corporate union. At first only the South India United Church and the Anglicans accepted the invitation. In 1925 the Methodist Church joined in. Others refrained, either on basic principle like the Roman Catholics, or because they had their own union problems nearer home, like the Thomas Christians, or because at that time they simply were not interested.

The path to union proved long and hard. There were few, if any, precedents. There was no case on record in which episcopal and non-episcopal churches had successfully come together; earlier efforts, such as those in South Africa, had hardly gotten beyond the preliminary stages. Those engaged in the long discussions in South India were most anxious not to create a new denomination which might lose such fellow-

---

12 *Ibid.*, p. 101.

ship as it already possessed with churches in other areas of Christendom. Hence the long and enthralling correspondence with experts in all parts of the world. The members of the joint committee in South India were themselves by no means lacking in theological competence; but with becoming modesty they desired to submit all their thinking and planning to the judgment of a wider church.

In 1929 the first draft of a scheme of union was ready. In some ways it was a better, because a simpler, scheme than that which finally found acceptance in 1945. Why, then, this long and exhausting period of delay? The answer is that throughout the long period of gestation the work of the joint committee on church union was subject to fierce criticism and even hostility from many sides.

Some radical Indian critics, such as Mr. V. Chakkarai and Mr. D. M. Devasahayam, maintained almost fanatically that the whole scheme was one which was being wished on the Indian churches by Western leaders; the problems discussed, they maintained, had nothing whatever to do with the interests of the Indian church or the mentality of the Indian Christian. It was clear that a united church fashioned by such Indian architects as these would retain no measure of fellowship at all with any other Christian body in the wide world. On the other hand, it must be remembered that the impulse to unity came from Indian Christians, and that many Indian leaders such as Bishop Azariah and Dr. (later Bishop) A. J. Appasāmy remained throughout the long period of more than twenty years devoted supporters of the union movement.

From some free churchmen came the criticism that the scheme was far too Anglican, and that by the acceptance of the episcopate the new church would in reality be a purely Anglican Church. What were the Anglicans giving up? One answer was that the Anglicans were giving up their place in the closely knit fellowship of the world-wide Anglican communion; their bishops would not be summoned to the Lambeth conference of Anglican bishops. On the other hand, rigid Anglicans criticized the scheme harshly as a betrayal of

Anglican principles, since it was provided that not all con-
firmations should be carried out by bishops only, and that
non-Anglican ministers would be permitted to carry on their
ministry in the new church without re-ordination.

A new generation of young Congregational missionaries
were extremely anxious lest their special principles might
be submerged by others which to them were of far less importance. At a late stage in the proceedings they proposed that,
as guarantee of the doctrine of the universal priesthood of
believers, lay celebration of the Holy Communion should be
permitted. This would have wrecked the scheme in its entirety.

Far on in the proceedings, a continental voice was heard
from the Basel Mission, objecting that the place of authority
given to the Holy Scriptures by no means guaranteed that the
new church would be and would remain a church of the
Reformation; the basic declaration had to be altered to satisfy
those who held this point of view.

At last all objections seemed to have been met, and in
1944 the churches were able to go forward with the elaborate
and highly democratic processes of voting on the scheme. In
its final form the scheme was based on the Scriptures as the
supreme authority in the life of the church, on the Apostles'
and Nicene Creeds as the authorized summary of the faith and
as the key to the interpretation of the Scriptures, on the
sacraments of baptism and the Lord's Supper, on the three-
fold ministry of the historic episcopate in constitutional form,
of presbyters and deacons, with at the same time a stress on
the function of the laity in the church, which up to that date
was unique in official church documents. One of the original
features of the scheme was the decision that all ministers in
good standing in any of the traditions should continue to
exercise their ministry in the new church without any form
of re-ordination, and should be eligible for election to the
episcopate; but that after thirty years the church should itself decide what exceptions, if any, it would make to the
rule of episcopal ordination. This last provision caused a
certain breach in relations with the Church of England, which

by the Act of Uniformity of 1662 is rigidly bound to an episcopal ministry and no other.[13]

In September 1947 the inauguration of the Church of South India took place in the Cathedral of St. George in Madras. In many ways it was a day of sadness; so many of the great architects of union, among them V. S. Azariah and Harry Waller, had passed to their reward and were not there. But sorrow was swallowed up in joy as the presiding bishop, C. K. Jacob of Travancore, declared that where there had been four churches now there was only one, the Church of South India, and 3,000 communicants from all the traditions joined in the Holy Communion. Nine new bishops, Indian and Western, Anglican, Presbyterian, Congregational and Methodist, were consecrated to serve the new church in its highest office. It was felt to be good that in the year of India's political independence it was possible to offer to the Indian people an Indian church, fully self-governing and independent of any other on the earth, in which the old Western names would be forgotten in the new unity, but which still desired to remain in fellowship with the widest possible range of Christian bodies in other parts of the earth.

THE INFLUENCE OF SOUTH INDIA

The interest of the world-wide church in the proceedings in South India was considerable, and no complete collection exists anywhere in the world of the gigantic literature, in the form of books, pamphlets and articles, representing every conceivable point of view, which was written about this church in the following twenty years. The sincerest sign of appreciation is seen in the fact that almost every plan of union that has been sketched out in any part of the world in these years shows deep marks of the influence of South India, from the abortive plan for union in Britain between the Church of England and the free churches in the 1920's to the scheme which should have come into effect in Nigeria in 1965. From an early date both Ceylon and North India were

---

[13] This restriction applies to the Church of England only and not to other parts of the Anglican communion.

developing plans for union, with the added complication that the Baptists, who were absent in South India, were ready to take part in the discussions. Here final success has not been achieved, in part because in neither of these areas did the churches feel able to accept the South Indian solution of an interim period during which the union would be consolidated and brought to completion.

In South India itself the chief success of the new church has been in its discussions with the Lutherans, through which over a period of ten years full agreement has been reached on all disputed points. At the time of writing, the Lutherans have not yet found a new home in the Church of South India; but this may be attributed rather to influences outside India than to disagreements on the spot.

The Church of South India is far from perfect. It is still too dependent on foreign leadership and on foreign money. It has shown no signs of a great development of spiritual vitality and evangelistic zeal. Many rural areas have remained almost wholly uninfluenced by the fact of union. The spirit of local faction and jealousy has not been exorcised by a new spirit of fellowship. There is very much still to be done. But the great importance of the Church of South India lies simply in the fact that it exists. Previously insurmountable barriers have been surmounted or broken down. A workable plan has been found for the union of churches which had remained in separation for centuries. One of the harshest criticisms of religion put forward by such Indian leaders as Pundit Jahawarlal Nehru is that religion always serves as a divisive force. Here for once it was possible to show Christian faith as a uniting force, through which men of different castes, backgrounds and traditions, separated for centuries in Hinduism, could be brought into a living unity with Jesus Christ and with one another, with an eager readiness to serve the new India which had obtained its political freedom in the same year in which the Church of South India came to birth.

VIII

THE CHURCH IN INDEPENDENT
INDIA AND PAKISTAN

ON AUGUST 15, 1947, THE LONG-PROMISED INDEPENDENCE BE-came a fact and the two new nations, India and Pakistan, were born. Each was to be fully independent, but each freely decided to remain with the British Commonwealth of Nations.

By 1947 it had become plain that, if independence was to come soon, partition was an inescapable necessity. But never in history has a partition been so difficult to achieve and so apparently unworkable. Pakistan exists in two separate units, divided by a thousand miles of Indian territory, with no mutual access except by air or sea, and with nothing to hold together the two widely differing sections other than the existence in both of a large Muslim majority. But, to add to the complications, forty million Muslims were left behind in India, to constitute the largest religious minority in that country. Apart from these permanent drawbacks, there were endless difficulties in the first years of adjustment. After a few weeks the deadly spirit of massacre and terrorism died down. But this was followed by a mass exodus in both di-rections, with all the resultant problems of the absorption of a large refugee population. The British had never even imagined the possibility of division. Everything — posts, rail, administration — had been organized on a unified basis. The majority even of the bank clerks in Pakistan were Hindus, who took the first opportunity to make their way out of the country. There was grave danger of chaos on both sides of the border.

With all these heavy tasks to shoulder, it might have been hoped that the two nations would have settled down in a spirit of friendly cooperation, to help one another out of the jungle of disorder into the new life of freedom. Unhappily this was far from being the case. The attitude of the two countries towards the separation was completely different. To the Indian, partition was something that ought never to have taken place, a rending of the unity of the body of Mother India, which had to be accepted as a concession to the Muslims in order that independence might be attained without delay, but not as a permanent solution to any problem. Many Indians are still convinced that sooner or later Pakistan will have to return to the unity of India, which ought never to have been broken. To the Pakistani, in contrast, the birth of the new state came as the inspiring realization of a dream; here was a state in which the Muslim could live freely as a Muslim, and work out what to him is the divinely appointed order for the life of man in this world. Many Pakistanis would rather die than return to an uneasy fellowship with a country which presents itself to them as primarily Hindustan, the home of the Hindus. To them partition is the first and great reality of existence.

Apart from this fundamental difference, relations between the two countries have from the start been bedeviled by a number of immediate problems.

The first arose from the simple fact that, for the water on which their life depends, large areas of Pakistan were dependent on rivers the headwaters of which are in Indian hands. The great series of dams and barrages, created by the British, through which millions of acres of desert had been turned into fertile fields, had all been planned on a unitary basis. If India could (and on one occasion it did) cut off

Pakistan's supply of water, fertile fields would return to desert. In one of the finest enterprises of international service ever recorded, the World Bank stepped in, planned the re-shaping of the whole scheme of irrigation, and made available large sums of money with the help of which new dams and canals could be created and the system organized on a dual and not a unitary basis. The work is not yet completed, but by the end of 1967 the new pattern was beginning to appear.

Less fortunate is the history of the other great ground of contention — the state of Kashmir. In 1947 the Hindu ruler of this state, with four million Muslim subjects, acceded to India without any kind of consultation with his people. For India, this settled the matter; by law Kashmir is part of India, and everything which affects Kashmir is part of the domestic politics of India in which no other country has any right to interfere. Pakistan has taken the line that, in these days of self-determination, these four million people ought to have some chance to say in which of the two states they would rather live. If, in a plebiscite held under the auspices of the United Nations, they declared themselves in favor of India, there would be nothing more to be said; but at least the possibility of joining with Pakistan should be open to them. Every attempt over twenty years to bring the two countries nearer to one another in this matter has been unsuccessful. In consequence 90 per cent of India's armed forces have sat along the frontiers of Pakistan, leaving the vulnerable frontier with China almost undefended. Inflamed feelings have led at least once to a short and abortive war. And, though one of India's bitterest complaints against Britain was the weight of expenditure on defense, India's defense budget today is heavier, as a proportion of the gross national product, than it ever was in British days.

It must truthfully be admitted that the great majority of Christians share in these matters the political outlook of the country of which they are citizens. But for all that, the church is the one body which has maintained its sense of unity across the new and bitter frontiers. It has been found necessary to create a new Christian Council of West Pakistan, another of East Pakistan. But both the Roman Catholic and Anglican churches, and perhaps others as well, have managed to maintain their organization intact. The Anglican Church is still the Church of India, Pakistan, Burma and Ceylon. How long, in face of increasing difficulties, it will be possible to maintain this unity, it must be left to history to decide. It may, however, be said without fear of contradiction, that Christians in the two countries have a stronger feeling of fellowship with one another than any other group, the Muslims not excepted.

THE CHRISTIAN SITUATION TODAY

We have noted the gradually changing attitude of Indian Christians towards the national movements. When the day of independence came, the minds of all had been thoroughly prepared for the change. Some accepted it with jubilation as the fulfillment of great hopes; others with some reluctance, fearing that liberties newly attained under the British would be jeopardized; perhaps the majority with acquiescence, as one of those things that happen in history without the ordinary man having very much to say on his own behalf. Whatever the mood or feeling, the new situation was accepted by all. Many missionaries, perhaps rather more than half, felt that the change had come too soon, and had been too radical; India might have gained much by another fifty years of cooperation with the British. The vast majority were opposed to the solution of partition. But once the decision had been taken, all accepted it; not one single missionary of any denomination relinquished his post on political grounds, or through unwillingness to accept the new situation as it had come upon him.

The two new countries were sharply divided in their attitude to religious questions, as in almost everything else.

India had declared itself to be a secular democratic republic. This has been interpreted to mean that the republic, while fully recognizing the significance of religion in the life of men, regards this whole realm as outside the range of its competence and interests, except in so far as public order may be affected, and will maintain even-handed impartiality in relation to all the existing religions. Some Indian leaders, such as the first Prime Minister, Mr. Nehru, would have been glad if all religions could have disappeared off the face of the earth; the majority retain at least nominal member-ship in one or other of the great religions of the past. Seeing their opportunity, the Christian members of the Constituent Assembly, by which the constitution of India was to be de-termined, came forward with a strong plea for a declaration of religious liberty to be included in that document. Although they were only a tiny minority, so skillful was their advocacy that an excellent declaration on the subject was included. In India today every citizen has the constitutional right to hold, to practice and to propagate any religion of the truth of which he is himself convinced. There may be infringements of this principle; the principle itself stands unchallenged.

Pakistan came into existence on the basis of a particular Muslim demand. Muslims had become convinced that they would not be able to exercise their own special vocation in a state mainly dominated by Hindus; they must have their own country, in which the Muslim faith would be a deter-mining political and social factor. This being so, complete im-partiality as between the religions was unthinkable. The first title of the new state was "the democratic Islamic republic of Pakistan." It was clearly stated that this was to be a state in which the Muslim could freely develop his own life ac-cording to the precepts of the holy Qur'an and of the *Shar'iah* (the traditional Islamic law). On the other hand, the ma-jority of the statesmen of Pakistan at the time of partition had studied in the West, had absorbed much of the spirit of Western democracy, and were concerned that differences of religious conviction should not be used as a basis for po-litical discrimination. There is, thus, an initial self-contra-diction in the principles on the basis of which Pakistan came into being; on the one hand the Muslim *Ulemā* (teach-ers) desired that everything should be ordered in a strictly Islamic way; the majority of politicians wished their country to take rank with all the other modern democracies in which the liberty of the individual is fully secured. Under their influence religious liberty has here too been written into the constitution, with a few limitations, such as the provision that the head of state must always be a Muslim.

Constitutional guarantees are an excellent thing; but much depends on the way in which the constitution is worked. To what extent can it be said that the Indian or Pakistani Christian has as much freedom as he had in the days before independence?

The educated Indian is prepared to accept the fact that a Christian community exists in India; as Mr. Nehru himself often pointed out, Christians were already in India before the Muslim faith came into existence. But he dislikes very much the idea of the increase of that community. To him the idea of conversion from one religious system to another out of personal conviction is unintelligible. In India religious and political community have gone so closely together that to become a Christian appears primarily to be a desertion of one social and political order and adhesion to another. Hence the cry that has constantly gone up, from Mr. Gāndhi among others, "Why cannot the Christian missionaries be content with their social and charitable work, without attaching to it the idea of conversion?" This being the view commonly held, it is natural that attempts at Christian conversion should be subjected to the closest scrutiny. A few years after independence, the so-called Nyogi report was published in Madhya Pradesh (the former Central Provinces). In this, under official sanction, all kinds of charges were made against the missionaries: exercising undue pressure on minors, holding out economic inducements and so on, in order to secure the maximum number of conversions.[1] The National Christian Council and Roman Catholic organizations had little difficulty in showing that many of these charges were fabrica-

---

[1] *Report of the Christian Missionary Activity Enquiry Committee, Madhya Pradesh, 1956* (Nagpur: Government Printing Press, 1956), 2 vols. In May 1968 an attempt was made to reactivate this long-since obsolete document.

tions, and that others referred to practices which had long since been abandoned by all conscientious missionaries. Nevertheless, the report served as a useful warning to both missionaries and Indian Christians that the service of the gospel can easily be corrupted by secondary motives, and that watchful care must be taken always to "provide things honest in the sight of all men."

It is at the point of the admission of missionaries that the new order has weighed hardest on the Christian cause. For a time missionaries from the Commonwealth countries could enter India without special permission; this privilege has now been withdrawn, and even Commonwealth citizens are most carefully scrutinized before permission to enter India is granted. Shortly before the time of writing a young Englishman who had qualified himself both in agriculture and in theology was appointed to an agricultural mission in Bihar. It might have been thought that agriculturalists are exactly the people most needed in India at the present time; nevertheless, in this case too, permission to reside in India was withheld, and the intending missionary had to transfer to Zambia. It is likely that such difficulties will increase rather than diminish in the future.

The usual charge against missionaries is that of having taken part in political activity, an odd change since the days in which exactly the opposite charge, that of being too little concerned with India's political development, was regularly bandied about. There are certain sensitive regions in India, especially in the tribal areas, where the influence of missionaries has been especially powerful. For instance, the formerly head-hunting Nāgas on the border between India and Burma owe almost everything that they have of civilization, not to mention the knowledge of the gospel, to the devoted work of American Baptists, who gave to them a sense of human dignity and a desire for independence far greater than the highly centralized government of India was prepared to grant. The question of Nāgaland has continued to perplex the government over many years; it is not surprising that, in consequence, access by missionaries to this area is forbidden, and

162   THE CHRISTIAN CHURCH IN INDIA AND PAKISTAN

many in high places would feel happy if the prohibition could be extended to the whole of India. In the week during which this chapter was written, an official statement of the government affirmed that the work of missionaries would be very carefully watched, and that any missionary found guilty of engaging in forbidden activities would find his service in India at an end.

The total number of missionaries in India has always been astonishingly small in proportion to the whole population. It seems clear that in the future the Indian church will have to become more and more dependent on its own resources, without expecting help from outside. This may be no bad thing; the disappearance of all missionaries from certain areas during the second world war was accompanied by great growth in the sense of responsibility on the part of Christians in the bereaved churches. Such responsibility must be extended beyond the maintenance of the existing church structure to the proclamation of the gospel in areas which have never previously been reached. It is of interest to note that the oldest missionary society of the Indian church, the Indian Missionary Society of Tirunelveli (founded in 1903), embarked in the year 1967 on an entirely new venture in a remote tribal area of Orissa, where nothing had ever previously been done. The first missionary to be appointed was not an ordained minister but a qualified veterinary surgeon.

In face of all the new difficulties — the growth of a stubborn Indian nationalism, the Hindu renaissance, at times vigorous opposition in official quarters — it might have been thought that the Indian church would have tended to diminish rather than to grow during the years since independence. Careful study shows that this is not so, and that even in these difficult days the church has continued to advance. The last census which provided fully reliable religious statistics for the country as a whole was that of 1931. From those figures it became clear that during the decade between 1921 and 1931, whereas the growth of the population as a whole had been a little more than 10 per cent, Christian growth had been 32 per cent. This was unevenly divided,

Roman Catholics having advanced at the rate of 16 per cent, and Protestants at the rate of 45 per cent. No such rapid progress can be recorded today. Yet study of the census figures for 1961 has shown that the church has not merely maintained its strength proportionately to the whole by natural increase at a time at which the population explosion is a source of anxiety to all friends of India, but has even managed slightly to increase it. The increase has been very slight, and even today the Christian membership does not exceed 3 per cent of the population; that any increase at all has taken place must be regarded as very encouraging.[2]

The situation in Pakistan is in some ways more difficult than in India. A Muslim atmosphere is never favorable to the extension of the church. Christians in Pakistan are far less numerous than in India. The majority of them were of Hindu or tribal origin, and when partition came would have preferred to emigrate to India. But poverty kept them where they were, often in the position of landless laborers, sometimes even poorer than they had been in the past. On the whole the principle of religious liberty has been observed. Christian workers, as in all Muslim countries, have to be very careful as to what they say and what they do. But opportunities for Christian witness are not lacking. The government of Pakistan is perhaps less unfriendly to the foreigner than that of India, and the missionary who has something to offer in the way of educational or medical expertise is likely still to be a welcome visitor.

AT HOME IN INDIA AND PAKISTAN

More important than outward circumstances, whether favorable or the reverse, is the inner attitude of the church to the situation in which it finds itself. Since independence Christians in both India and Pakistan have made it clear that

---

2 It is very difficult to get accurate statistics of Christians and churches in Asian countries. It is probable that at the time of writing there are 13 million Christians in India, and rather more than a million in Pakistan. The *World Christian Handbook 1968* gives for Protestants: India, 5,303,206 (communicants 2,087,927); Pakistan, 472,997 (communicants 176,754).

they desire to be, and to be recognized as being, in the fullest sense of the term citizens of their new countries.

In earlier days the attitude of Christians towards political life was hesitant and reserved. Gradually it came home to Christians that this too was a sphere in which God could be glorified, and that to shrink from the difficulties was unworthy of a Christian man. Since independence Christians have taken a leading part in every sphere of central, provincial and local government. The first governor of Bombay after independence was a devout Anglican lay-reader, Rajah Sir Maharaj Singh, whose sister, the Rajkumari Amrit Kaur, was the first minister of health for the whole of India. A Baptist, Dr. H. C. Mukerjee, has been governor of West Bengal. The names of those who have served in less eminent posts make a long roll of honor.

Even more important than this political engagement is a new attitude on the part of Christians towards the classic cultures and the other religions of their countries.

The change has been specially notable in the Roman Catholic Church. As we have noted, steps towards the formation of an Indian clergy and episcopate were taken only grudgingly, and finally only under impulses from missionary-minded popes. The training of the Indian priest differed in no respect from that current in the West, and hardly any account was taken of the fact that, once ordained, the candidate would be working in an Indian language, and in the midst of people whose outlook was determined by a non-Christian religion and culture. When independence came, a majority of the Roman Catholic bishops were still foreigners. Since that date change has been rapid. New sees have been created, from the beginning under Indian leadership. Most of the famous bishoprics now have Indian incumbents. In 1950 the first full council of Indian bishops was held at Bangalore, under the presidency of Cardinal Gilroy, Archbishop of Sydney. In 1953 Mgr. Valerian Gracias, Archbishop of Bombay, was created Cardinal, the first Indian to receive that honor. The Roman Catholic Church in India was losing its foreignness, and beginning to take its place as a church fully at home on the soil of India.

Christians have at different times taken up various attitudes towards non-Christian religions. In early days the view of most missionaries was entirely negative: these religions are simply the invention of the devil to deceive men and lead them away from the heavenly Father. From about 1875 onwards this severe attitude began to change, and to be replaced by interest in, and sometimes an enthusiastic respect for, the ancient Asian forms of wisdom. In all except very conservative circles, it is accepted generally by Christians in India and Pakistan that they should know their own languages well and correct the tendency towards a Christian jargon which was marked in the nineteenth century, that they must be interested in the traditional culture of the country, and that they must try to enter with sympathy into the experiences of their non-Christian fellow citizens.

On the Protestant side the main center for study and research has been Bangalore, with its society for the study of the relations between church and society, and also its society for the study of Hinduism, now combined in the Christian Institute for the Study of Religions and Society. In Dr. Paul Devanandan, a Lutheran from an old Christian family, the Protestant churches found a prophet and champion of the new approach. Devanandan, having grown up in a Christian home, had not the inner knowledge of the Hindu world which is naturally possessed by the convert; but by patient study and deep sympathy he worked himself deeply into an understanding of what Hinduism means to the modern Hindu. Writing and study were supplemented by personal conversation, through which, as he grew older, Devanandan was himself brought to understand more fully the place that the church plays as a part of the Christian revelation, and to understand the difficulty that the Hindu experiences when faced with the challenge of a religious community other than his own. Jesus Christ he can accept as teacher, as ideal, even in some sense as mediator. That allegiance to Jesus will involve him also in fellowship with all the other disciples of

Jesus, a fellowship that finds its natural expression in the Holy Communion — this is the thing that is most difficult for him to accept. The early death of Paul Devanandan in 1963 was a serious loss to the Christian church in India.

On the Roman Catholic side, a change in outlook began with the work of Fr. Johanns, a Jesuit in Calcutta, who had received his training in Indology at Oxford.[3] Whereas for a long time Roman Catholic missionaries had despised the wisdom of India, Johanns had become convinced, through careful study of the ancient classics, that they contained much wisdom and truth, and that in a very real sense the Upanisads could serve as a preparation for the coming of Christ; not that they could replace the Old Testament, but that they could set the Hindu to asking questions, to which the answer would be found only in Jesus Christ. "To Christ by way of the Vedanta" is the title of a series of articles in the periodical *The Light of the East*. The most notable successor of Johanns today is another scholar, Fr. Raymond Panikkar, the son of an Indian father and a Spanish mother, who in his book translated under the title *The Unknown Christ of Hinduism*[4] has set forth the somewhat paradoxical view that the task of Christianity in India is neither to detach individuals from Hinduism nor to destroy the ancient faith, but to annex it; Christ is already in a sense present in Hinduism; the Hindu must be helped to develop within Hinduism explicit faith in the Christ, after whom he is searching, and whom in some dim sense he already knows.

There is always a danger, in such amicable approaches to men of other faiths, that the essential content of the gospel may be lost or watered down. Yet it can hardly be doubted that this open and friendly attitude of the Christian will help to disarm the prejudices of the non-Christian, and may help

---

3 Reference should perhaps also be made to the work of Fr. William Wallace, a former missionary of the Church Missionary Society in Bengal who had become a Jesuit. He believed that a good knowledge of Hinduism was essential equipment for a successful approach to the higher castes in India.

4 With extensive bibliography.

to lead on to that open dialogue, in which the truth of God as revealed in Jesus Christ may become evident to the minds of all who truly seek him.

AND WHAT OF THE FUTURE?

We have traveled a long way through time together. We have seen the first birth of an Indian church many centuries ago. We have watched it through the ebb and flow of time, often isolated, weakened, apparently crushed, yet always rising again to new extensions and new victories of grace. How shall we estimate the present position and the future prospects of the church of Jesus Christ in India and Pakistan?

Considering the length of the period during which Christian missions have been carried on, and the immense devotion poured into the work by armies of Christian workers, it might seem that the success achieved has been trivial. The Indian writer and diplomat K. N. Panikkar, in his book *Asia and Western Dominance,* has put forward clearly and harshly the view that Christian missions came into Asia as the handmaid of the domination of the Western powers, that they have never really touched the hearts of the Asian peoples, and that with the withdrawal of colonialism they will run into inescapable collapse. It seems hardly likely that he is right. It is true that numbers are small, barely 3 per cent in India and less than 1 per cent in Pakistan. Yet these small minorities are well grounded and show every sign of having taken root in the soil of the subcontinent. It can be maintained with some confidence that, if every foreign missionary and every cent of foreign support were withdrawn, the churches, though weakened at certain points, would still maintain their existence, and would continue to expand, though perhaps more slowly than in the past. The number of fully independent and self-governing churches has increased rapidly in recent years. Most of the leading positions in the churches are filled by nationals. The faith of the village Christian is in many cases unenlightened, but it is real; it is most unlikely that he will ever forsake this religion in favor of any other. The enormous educational effort of the nineteenth century has taken effect. Christians in spite of the humble origins of the majority among them are, after Parsis and Brahmans, the best-educated community in India. This means that their influence is out of all proportion to their numbers. And, although the way in which Christians live is often very different from what it ought to be, non-Christians understand very well what is meant by Christian standards, and criticize Christians harshly in the light of that gospel which they profess to believe. Perhaps they are themselves challenged to some extent by standards whose relevance they admit, though they do not accept the sources from which those standards are derived.

The present is somewhat stable. What of the future? Of this naturally it is possible to speak only with great caution. We have seen something of the new difficulties with which Christians are faced in both countries and the probability that those difficulties may increase. The observer is inclined to think at times that the churches are marked today rather by a certain timid passivity than by the spirit of resolution and adventure which ought to be called out by a difficult situation. Neither the coming of independence, nor such great steps forward as the formation of the Church of South India, have led to a great release of new spiritual power. An Indian observer from East Africa, returning on leave to his own country, wrote especially of the Protestant churches that they seem hardly aware of the new possibilities for Christian witness that exist in the India of today.[5] It is true that the witness for Christ in India and Pakistan must be cautious and anxious not to offend. But he is far from being the only one who is perplexed by the new situation. Now that India and Pakistan have been independent long enough for the first glow to have faded and for the disappointment of many hopes and expectations to become a painful reality, many

---

[5] See Din Dayal, "Defeatist Protestantism and Open Doors in India," *International Review of Missions* (1960), pp. 446-449, esp. p. 449: "The contrast between retreating Protestantism and advancing Roman Catholicism is too obvious to be missed. The Protestant missions and churches must search their hearts. Are they right in deserting their responsibilities in fear?"

in both countries are looking round for such a faith as could become a source of ethical renewal and spiritual power, to be used in the exacting service of two great but poor and underdeveloped countries.

Almost every educated person in India or Pakistan has some knowledge of Jesus Christ. The great majority have a deep reverence for his person and his teaching. India is ready to accept Jesus Christ as "one of the Saviors of mankind." The way from this affirmation to the confession of Jesus Christ as the last word of God to man, and as the one through whom men draw near to the Father, is very long. But it is only through the church in these countries, weak, imperfect and in part ineffective as all human instruments are, that the many peoples of India and Pakistan will find the way. This is the task to the fulfillment of which the churches have to gird themselves in the last third of the twentieth century.

BIBLIOGRAPHY

Appasāmy, A. J. *Indian Christian Poet.* (World Christian Books, no. 56.) London: U. S. C. L., Lutterworth Press, 1966.
———. *Sadhu Sundar Singh.* London: Lutterworth Press, 1958.
Ariarajah, S. Wesley, "Chenchiah's Christology," *Bangalore Theological Forum,* no. 1, 1968.
Barber, Noel. *The Black Hole of Calcutta.* London: Collins, 1965.
Barclay, W. C. *History of Methodist Missions.* New York: Board of Missions and Church Extension of the Methodist Church, 1949. This missionary society history is one of exceptional value; India is dealt with in vol. 3: *Expanding Horizons* (1957), pp. 451-649.
Brodrick, J., S.J. *Saint Francis Xavier.* London: Burns, Oates, 1952.
Brown, L. W. *The Indian Christians of St. Thomas.* Cambridge: University Press, 1956. The reader will find here most of what he needs for the early period and for the history of the Thomas Christians.
Buchanan, C. *Christian Researches in Asia; with notices of the Translation of the Scriptures into the Oriental Languages.* 9th ed. London: Cadell and Davies, 1812.
Bühlmann, P. *Anastasius Hartmann.* Fribourg, 1965.
Burnell, A. C. in *Cambridge History of India,* vol. 5. Cambridge: University Press, 1929.
Caldwell, R. *The Early History of the Tinnevelly Mission.* Madras: Higginbotham, 1881.
Carey, S. Pearce. *William Carey.* London: Hodder and Stoughton, 1925.
Chatterton, E. *A History of the Church of England in India since the Early Days of the East India Company.* London: S. P. C. K., 1924. This book is still the best authority on Anglican work in India.
Cronin, V. *A Pearl to India: the Life of Robert de Nobili.* London: Hart-Davies, 1959.
Dayal, Din, "Defeatist Protestantism and Open Doors in India," *International Review of Missions,* 1960.

Digby, W. *The Famine Campaign in Southern India*, 2 vols. London: Longmans, 1878.

Farquhar, J. N. *Modern Religious Movements in India*. New York: Macmillan, 1915. This book is still the classic work on movements of reform and renewal within the Indian religions.

Firth, C. B. *An Introduction to Indian Church History*. (The Christian Students' Library, no. 23.) Madras: C.L.S., 1961. With the single reservation that the earlier part of the story is more fully dealt with than the later, this one simple book can be recommended for the Christian history of India.

Foster, John, "The Four Martyrs of Thana 1321," *International Review of Missions*, XLVI (1956), 204-208.

Gensichen, H. W., " 'Abominable Heathenism'; A rediscovered tract by Bartolomaeus Ziegenbalg," *Indian Church History Review*, I, no. 1 (1967), 29ff.

Goodall, N. *A History of the London Missionary Society 1895-1945*. Oxford, 1954.

Graham, C. *Azariah of Dornakal*. London: S. C. M. Press, 1947.

Grimes, C. J. *Towards an Indian Church*. London: S.P.C.K., 1946. This is a thorough and interesting study of the way in which a Western-controlled church became a genuinely Indian church.

Hill, W. D. P., trans. *Bhagavad Gītā*. Oxford: University Press, 1953.

Hodne, O. L. C. *Skrefsrud, Missionary and Social Reformer among the Santals*. Oslo, 1966.

Hough, J. *The History of Christianity in India*, vol. 2. London: Seely, 1839.

International Review of Missions. For those who wish to follow the course of events in India since 1947, the best method is to take the annual survey of the Christian world published each year in January by the *International Review of Missions*. This periodical also publishes regularly a classified and reliable bibliography of missionary literature, through which the student of missions can easily keep in touch with what is going on in the church in India and Pakistan.

"The Invalidity of the Synod of Diamper," *Indian Church History Review*, I, no. 1 (1967), 9ff.

Latourette, K. S. *History of the Expansion of Christianity*, 7 vols. New York and London: Harper and Brother, 1937-1945. This great work has the following sections on Christianity in India: vol. 1, pp. 231-233; vol. 2, pp. 280-284; vol. 3, pp. 247-284; vol. 6, pp. 65-214; vol. 7, pp. 274-315.

Lehmann, A. *Alte Briefe aus Indien, 1706-1719*. Berlin: Evang. Verlag, 1957.

———. *It Began in Tranquebar*. Madras: C. L. S., 1956. For the work of the Lutheran mission in the eighteenth century, this is the best introductory work.

Locke, J. C. *The First Englishmen in India*. London: Routledge, 1930.

Macnicol, N. *Living Religions of the Indian People*. New ed. revised by

M. H. Harrison. New Delhi: Y.M.C.A., 1965. This is the best simple book for the religious background of the Indian people.

———. *Pandita Ramabai*. Calcutta: Y. M. C. A., 1926.

Majumdar, R. C., Raychaudhuri, H. C., and Datta, K. *An Advanced History of India*. 10th reprint. London: Macmillan, 1963. This book of three Indian writers may be recommended for those who are prepared to tackle a larger and more exacting work than those of P. Spear.

Malleson, Col., C. S. I. *Dupleix. (Rulers of India* series.) Oxford: Clarendon Press, 1890.

Marshman, J. C. *The Life and Times of Carey, Marshman, and Ward*, 2 vols. London: Longmans, 1859.

Matthew, C. P., and Thomas, M. M. *The Indian Christians of Saint Thomas*. New Delhi: I. S. P. C. K., 1967. This recent book by two Indian authors deals primarily with the Mar Thoma Church.

Padwick, C. E. *Henry Martyn, Confessor of the Faith*. London: S. C. M. Press, 1922.

Panikkar, K. N. *Asia and Western Dominance*. London, 1953.

Panikkar, Raymond. *The Unknown Christ of Hinduism*. London: Darton, Longman and Todd, 1964.

Paton, W. *Alexander Duff, Pioneer of Missionary Education*. London: S. C. M. Press, 1922.

Paul, R. D. *Chosen Vessels*. (Christian Students' Library, no. 25.) Madras: C.L.S., 1961.

———. *The First Decade*. London: Lutterworth Press, 1950.

———. *Triumphs of His Grace*. Madras: C.L.S., 1967.

Pearson, Hugh. *Memoir of the life and correspondence of the Reverend Frederick Schwartz*, 2 vols. London: Hatchard, 1834.

Penny, F. *The Church in Madras*. London: Smith, Elder, 1904.

Pope, G. U. *The Tirukurral*. London: W. H. Allen & Co., 1886.

Popley, H. A. *K. T. Paul: Christian Leader*. Calcutta: Y. M. C. A., 1938.

Radhakrishnan, S. *Eastern Religions and Western Thought*. 2nd ed. Oxford: University Press, 1940. This book and the following one, as well as other works by Radhakrishnan, give a restatement of Hinduism.

———. *The Hindu View of Life*. 7th ed. London: Macmillan, 1948.

Report of the Christian Missionary Activity Enquiry Committee, Madhya Pradesh, 1956, 2 vols. Nagpur: Government Press, 1956.

Samartha, S. J. *Radhakrishnan: An Introduction to his Thought*. Bangalore: CISRS, 1966. Compare this critical introduction to the thought of Radhakrishnan by a Christian scholar, with the works of Radhakrishnan himself.

Sarma, D. S. *The Renaissance of Hinduism*. Benares: Hindu University, 1944.

Schurhammer, G., S.J. *Franz Xaver*. Freiburg: Herder, 1955, 1963. This great work, in German only, is the classic life of Xavier; vol. 2 deals with the work of Xavier in India.

Sherring, M. A. *The Indian Church during the Great Rebellion.* 2nd ed. London: James Nisbet, 1859.

Spear, P. *India.* Ann Arbor: University of Michigan Press, 1961. For the history of India in general, against the background of which the special Christian history must be studied, this is the most useful book for the ordinary reader.

———. *India, Pakistan and the West.* Oxford: Home University Library, 1947. This short book by the same author, in the Home University Library, is clear, well-balanced and full of matter.

Stevenson, Mrs. Sinclair. *Rites of the Twice-born.* Humphrey Milford: Oxford University Press, 1920.

Stock, E. *The History of the Church Missionary Society,* 3 vols. London: C. M. S., 1899. This missionary society history is also of exceptional value.

Sundkler, B. G. M. *The Church of South India.* London: Lutterworth Press, 1954. On the formation of the Church of South India, this is the classic work.

Thangasamy, D. A. *The Theology of Chenchiah.* Bangalore: CISRS, 1967.

Tilak, L. *From Brahma to Christ.* (World Christian Books, no. 9.) London: U. S. C. L., Lutterworth Press, 1956.

Wheeler, Sir Mortimer. *Rome beyond the Imperial Frontiers.* Harmondsworth: Penguin Books, 1952.

Wicki, J. *Documenta Indica,* 11 vols. Rome: Monumenta Historica Soc. Iesu, 1948-1969.

Wilson, D. C. *Dr. Ida: the Story of Dr. Ida Scudder of Vellore.* New York, 1958.

Wolff, O. *Christus unter den Hindus.* Gütersloh: Gerd Mohn, 1965. For those who can read German, this book is full of material based on original sources.

Yesudhas, D., "Indigenization or Adaptation," *Bangalore Theological Forum,* II (1967), 39-52.

INDEX

Aaron, first ordained Indian, 56
Abbanes, 17
Abraham, Mar, 35
Act of Uniformity, 153
Afras, 20
Agliardi, Mgr., 109
Agni, 13
Agra, 97, 108f.
Agricultural Institute, 97
Ahatalla, 36
Ahimsā, 131
Akbar, 28, 37
Alam, Shah, 85
Albuquerque, 29
Alexander the Great, 12
Ali, Haidar, 59
Allahabad, 96f.
Ambedkar, B. R., 14n.
America (United States of), 75, 96, 99, 125f., 138, 140, 149
Amritsar, 77, 130f.
Anderson, Rufus, 138
Andrews, Charles Freer, 132
Angamalle, 33
Anglicans, 82, 86, 101, 107f., 140, 150f.
Anne, Queen of England, 55
Aphroth, Mar (Prod), 20
Appasāmy, A. J., 142n., 151
Arabia, 18
Arcot, 75; South Arcot, 98
Ariarajah, S. Wesley, 143n.
Arikkamedu, Roman settlement, 16
Arjuna, 15
Armenians, 38
Aryans, 12, 15

Ārya Samāj, 123f.
āshram, 144
  Christa Prema Seva Sangh, 144
  Christa Seva Sangh, 144
  Christukula *Āshram*, 145
Asia, 21, 28, 49, 146
Assam, 79
Athanasius, Matthew, 106f.
Athanasius, Thomas, 107
Ātman, 14
Augustinians, 41
Attlee, Clement, 134
Azariah, Vedanayakam Samuel, 136, 151, 153
Azores, 41

Bābu, 129
Bābur, 27
Babylon, 18
Bailey, Benjamin, 83
Baker, Henry, 83
Baldaeus, Philippus, 52
Baluchistan, 16
Bangalore, 164f.; Bangalore Conference, 146
Bangor, 50
Bannu, 96
Barber, Noel, 51n.
Bareilly, 96, 98
Baroda, 98
Barton, John, 138f.
Belgium, 101
Bellamy, Gervas, 51
Bengal, 49, 64, 67, 76, 101f., 117, 124, 135; Bengalis, 100, 121
Bentinck, William, 66
Berlin, 70

Beschi, Constantius Joseph, 40, 55
Bhagavad Gītā, 15, 25, 31
Bhakti, 15, 25
Bharathas, 30
Bhils, 102
Bible, The, 47, 70, 146
  Holy Scriptures, 46f., 67, 116, 152
  Old Testament, 56, 117, 143, 166
  New Testament, 46f., 54ff., 68,
    83, 117, 131, 140
Bihar, 101, 161
Bishop's College, Calcutta, 76, 136
Black Hole of Calcutta, 50
Böhme, Anton Wilhelm, 55f.
Bombay, 49, 73, 75, 79, 86, 108f.,
  111
Bonnand, Mgr., Bishop of Pondi-
  cherry, 108
Book of Common Prayer, 58, 140
Booth-Tucker, Frederick, 99
Børresen, H. P., 101
Brahman, 38, 42, 117, 119f., 168
  Brahman, 14
  Brahman priesthood, 13
Brahmiya-Samāj, 119f.
Brahmo Covenant, 119
Brahmo Samāj, 120
Braithwaite, 74
Brazil, 40
Brésillac, Gaston de Marion, 87
Bristol, 119
Britain, 49, 63, 178; *see* Great
  Britain
British, 49, 52, 110, 155f., 158
British Commonwealth of Nations,
  155, 161
British Empire, 130
Britto, John de, 40
Brother Jordan, 22f.; *see* Séverac
Brown, Edith, 97
Buchanan, Claudius, 82
Buddha, 14; Buddhism, 14f.
Burma, 102, 161
Burnell, A. C., 53

Cadi, 22
Caesarius, Johannes, 52

Calcutta, 49, 52f., 65, 67, 72, 76, 85,
  96, 100, 108f., 111, 116-120 *pas-
  sim*, 131, 136, 139, 166
Caldwell, R., 61n.
Calicut, 27
Calvinism, 65
Cambridge, University of, 127
Canara, South, 77
Cannanore, 78
Canning, "Clemency," 89
Canoz, Alexis, 111
Cape Comorin, 11, 30, 61, 64
Capuchins, 86
Carey, William, 66, 68f., 75
Castro, Matthew de, 42f.
Cathay, 41
Ceylon, 18, 75, 109, 153
Chakkarai, V., 143, 151
Charbonneaux, Mgr., Bishop of
  Mysore, 108
Charles II of England, 49f.
Charnock, Job, 49
Chenchiah, P., 143
Chicago, 125
China, 21f., 41, 102, 157
Chinsurah, 52
Chitambar, J. R., 137
Chota Nagpur, 100f.
Christian Councils of East Paki-
  stan and West Pakistan, 158
Christian Institute for the Study
  of Religions and Society, 165
Chuhra, 104f.
Churches, missions and societies
  American Baptists, 102, 104, 154,
    161
  American Board of Commission-
    ers for Foreign Missions, 75
  American Dutch Reformed, 75
  American Lutherans, 98
  American Methodist Episcopal
    Church, 98
  American Methodists, 96, 140
  American Presbyterians, 76, 96
  Basel Mission, 77, 97, 152
  British Methodists, 141
  Church Missionary Society, 70,

76f., 82, 98, 138
Church of England (Anglican Church), 86, 106, 108, 150, 152f.
Church of England Zenana Missionary Society, 94
Church of India, Burma and Ceylon, 140
Church of India, Pakistan, Burma and Ceylon, 158
Church of Scotland, 72
Church of South India, 153f., 168
Congregational Church, 148f.
Danish Mission, 98
Danish Royal Mission, 53, 55, 57, 60, 78
English Baptists, 102, 154
Irish Presbyterians, 79, 81
London Missionary Society, 71, 79, 96
Lutheran Leipzig Mission, 78f.
Societas Fratrum Peregrinantium propter Christus inter Gentes, 21
Société des Missions Etrangères, 43, 46
Society for the Promotion of Christian Knowledge, 56, 58
Society of Jesus, 30
Syrian Church, 83
United Presbyterian Mission, 97
Welsh Presbyterians, 79, 102
Zenana Bible and Medical Mission, 94
Clive, Robert, 63
Clough, John E., 104
C.M.S. College in Kottayam, 83
Cochin, 29, 33, 35, 44, 49
Coimbatore, 87
Coimbra, 36n.
College of St. Francis Xavier (Calcutta), 111
College of St. Joseph (Trichinopoly, 111
College of St. Paul (Goa), 32, 37, 43, 46
Colombo, 49

Concordat of 1801, 84
Congregation for the Oriental Churches, 109
Congress Party, 132ff.
Constituent Assembly, 159
Copenhagen, 53
Coromandel Coast, 30
Corrie, Daniel, 76
Cotton, Bishop, 140
Counter-reformation, 34, 39, 44, 48
Cruikshank, 73
Cuddalore, 49, 58

Dacca, 108
da Gama, Vasco, 27f.
Dalhousie, Lord, 91
Danes, 49, 53, 101
Dasyus, 15
Datta, K., 27n.
Dayal, Din, 168n.
Delhi, 27, 62
Denmark, 56
Dera Ghazi Khan, 96
Devanandan, Paul, 165
Devasahayam, D. M., 151
Devasahayam, John, 71
Diamper, 35
Diaz, Bartholomew, 28
Digby, W., 92n.
Dilbar, Hans, 101
Din Illahi, 37
Dionysius III, Metropolitan, 83
Dionysius IV, Metropolitan, 83
Ditt, 104
Doab, 85
Dominicans, 21f.
Dominus ac Redemptor, 45
Dornakal diocese, 137
Doyabari, 96
Dravidians, 15, 102; *see also* pre-Dravidian people
Dubois, Abbé, 79
Duff, Alexander, 72f., 75, 116, 118
Dupleix, Joseph François, 62
Dutch, The, 44, 49, 52f., 82
Dyer, General, 130f.

East India Company (British), 49ff., 58f., 63f.; charter of, 64, 67, 75, 88f., 92, 117
Edinburgh, 72, 146
Egypt, 16, 123
England, 66, 68, 119
Europe, 12, 24, 28, 44, 48f., 55, 57, 64, 75, 82, 123
Evangelicals, 65
Evans, John, 51

Fabricius, Philip, 56, 58, 146
Farquhar, J. N., 119n.
Fenn, Joseph, 83
Fisher Coast, 32f., 46, 137
Forman, Charles W., 76
Forrester-Paton, 144
Fort St. David, 49
Fort St. George, 49
Foster, John, 22n.
France, 43, 49, 63, 84, 86f.
Franciscans, 21f.
Francke, August Hermann, 53
Frederick IV, King of Denmark, 53
French Revolution, 84

Gāndhi, Mohandas Karamchand, Mahātmā, 116, 131-134 passim, 160
Ganges, 77, 85, 100
Gautama, 14; see Buddha
Genealogy of the Malabarian Gods, The, 57
Gensichen, W., 56n.
Gentilismus Reseratus, 53
George V, King, 130
Gericke, 58
Germann, Wilhelm, 57
Germany, 49, 53, 100
Gilroy, Cardinal, Archbishop of Sydney, 164
Gingee, 91
Goa, 29-47 passim, 85; Archbishop of, 108; schism of, 86, 109
Goes, Bento de, 41
Golden Temple, 77

Gonds, 102
Goreh, Nehemiah, 122
Gossner Mission, 100
Gracias, Valerian, 164
Grant, Charles, 65
Graul, Karl, 79
Great Britain, 89, 93; see Britain
Greece, 123; Greeks, 13
Gujerat, 98
Gundaphorus, 17
Gundobar, 17

Halle, 53f., 56n., 57
Hartman, Anastasius, 86
Heber, Reginald, 76
Hebich, Samuel, 78
Henriquez, Henry, 33n.
Henry the Navigator, Prince, 28
Higginbottom, Sam, 97
Hill, W. D. P., 15n., 132n.
Himalayas, 11, 12
Hinduism, 13, 15, 67, 69, 77f., 115f., 117-125 passim, 143, 154, 165
Hindus, 13-19 passim, 33-39 passim, 57, 70-124 passim, 134, 156
Hindustani, 59
Hindu Theistic Church, 119
Hislop, Stephen, 73
Holland, 49
Holland, Henry, 96
Holland, W. E. S., 147n.
Hortus Malabaricus, 52
Hos, 100
Hough, James, 69, 71
Hyderabad, 98, 108

Ibrahim, Sultan, 27
Independence, 155
India, 155-169 passim
Indian Civil Service, 77, 90, 99, 128
Indian Missionary Society of Tirunelveli, 136, 162
Indian National Congress, 130
Indian Ocean, 28
Indicopleustes, Cosmas, 17f.
Indonesia, 52
Ingoli, Francesco, 42

Iran, 16
Islam, 37, 80, 115, 117
Ismail, Mirza, 132
Italians, 24

Jacob, C. K., 84, 153
Jallianwala Bagh, 131
Jamshedpur, 93
Japanese, The, 133
Jehangir, 38
Jerusalem, 17
Jesudāson, 144
Jesuits (Society of Jesus), 29n., 30, 32, 33n., 35-45 *passim*, 101; Order dissolved, 45; Order reestablished 84; weaknesses, 46
Jinnah, Mohammed Ali, 133
Johanns, Fr., 166
John of Monte Corvino, 21
Jones, Stanley, 131
Joseph, Pulikot (Dionysius V), 107
Jubbulpore, 136
Juggernaut, 64
Jumna, 85
Justin Martyr, 25

Kanpur, 98
Karachi, 98
Karma, 14, 124
Kashmir, 11, 157
Kathiawar, 79, 122
Kaur, Rājkumāri Amrit, 164
Kerala, 11, 17, 47, 107
Khan, The Great, 21
Khanbalik (Peking), 22
Khasi hills, 79, 102
Khonds, The, 102
Khyber Pass, 64
Kierkels, Apostolic Delegate, 137
Kipling, Rudyard, 92, 102
Kohloff, 60
Kohloffs, The, 76
Kolarian people (the Kols), 100f.
Kollam, 16
Koonen cross, 36, 81
Kolumbum, 16
Kottayam, 83, 106

Kraemer, Hendrik, 143
Krishna, 15

Lahore, 4, 76
Lancashire, 93
Langhans, Ernst Friedrich, 78
Languages: *Eastern*: Arabic, 68, 117; Bengali, 67, 72, 119; Chinese, 67; Hebrew, 117; Hindustani, 59; Konkani, 43; Malayalam, 83; Marathi, 67, 142; Persian, 68, 117; Sanskrit, 12, 16, 38, 55, 58, 67, 117, 144; Santali, 101; Syriac, 83; Tamil, 15f., 18, 25, 31, 41, 55, 59, 70, 79; Urdu, 68; *Others:* English, 72, 117, 119; Greek, 117, 144; Portuguese, 51, 59
Larsen, L. P., 135
Lawrences, The, 90
Lehmann, Arno, 54
Leonard College, Jubbulpore, 136
Lievens, Constant, 101
Ling, Catherine, 103
Locke, J. C., 43n.
London, 55, 65, 116, 138
Loyola, Ignatius, 30, 32
Lucas, C. J., 148
Lucknow, 95, 98
Ludhiana, 97
Lushai hills, 102
Lutheran Church of Chota Nagpur and Assam, 100
Lutherans, 41, 54, 58, 98, 101, 136f., 148, 154, 165
Lütkens, Franz Julius, 53

Macassar, 49
Mādiga, 104
Madras, 11, 19, 21, 58f., 74, 85, 99, 104f., 109, 111f., 139, 153
Madras Christian College, 74
Madras Conference, 146, 147
Madura, 38ff., 73, 75
Madya Pradesh (Central Provinces), 160
Mahātmā Gāndhi, 116; *see* Gāndhi

Majumdar, R. C., 27n.
Malabar rites, 45
Malankara Church, 36, 81, 107
Mālas, 104
Malaya, 29
Male, 18
Malleson, C. S. I., 63n.
Malpan, Abraham, 106
Mangalore, 77
Mar Thoma Syrian Church, 107
Marathi, 59
Mardin, 106
Marignolli, John de, 23f.
Marshman, Joshua C., 65n., 66n., 67, 68n., 118
Martyn, Henry, 68, 76
Masulipatam, 73
Mattancerri, 36
Mayiladi, 71
Meath, 51
Mecca, 20
Medical Missions Training Institute, 97
Medina, 20
Megnanapuram, 71
Menezes, Aleixo de, 34ff.
Meriah, 102
Mesopotamia, 34, 82
Methodist Church of Southern Asia, 137, 141, 150
Methodists, 98, 105, 136
Middleton, Thomas F., 76
Miller, William, 112
Milman, Bishop, 100
Mogul, The Great, 37, 50
Mogul empire, 28, 37
Moguls, 28, 128
Mohenjo-Dāro, 12
Monro, James, 90, 96
Montague-Chelmsford reforms, 130
Montgomery, 90
Mooney, Apostolic Delegate, 137
Mother India, 134, 156
Mott, John R., 146
Mountbatten, Lord, 134
Muhammad, 20, 22

Mukerjee, H. C., 164
Müller, Max, 38, 120
Mundas, 100
Munro, Colonel, 82
Murshidabad, 117
Muslims, 20-28 passim, 37, 86-95 passim, 112, 115, 133f., 155-160 passim
Mylapore, 29
Mysore, 59, 63, 108, 132

Nadars, 61
Nadiya, 76, 77
Nāgaland, 161
Nāgas, 102, 161
Nagpur, 73, 98
Nāth, Narendra, 124f.; see Vivekānanda, Swāmi
National Christian Council of India, 133, 147, 160
National Missionary Conference, 146
Negapatam, 52, 111
Nehru, Jahawarlal, 132, 134, 154, 159f.
Nestorians, 22f.; Nestorian heresy, 18, 34
Neyyoor, 96
Nigeria, 153
Nilgiri hills, 102
Nizam, The, 98
Nobili, Robert de, 38f., 45, 55, 73, 75, 78, 114
Noble, Robert, 73
North India, 153
North India School of Medicine, 97
Norway, 49
Norwegians, 101
Nyogi Report, 160

Oblates of Mary Immaculate, 85
Oraons, 100
Orders, religious, 41, 145
    Augustinians, q.v.
    Capuchins, q.v.
    Carmelites, q.v. (Spanish)
    Dominicans, q.v.

Franciscans, q.v.
Jesuits, q.v.
Oblates of Mary Immaculate, q.v.
Salesians, q.v.
Orissa, 102, 162
Oxford, 120, 166
Oxford Mission to Calcutta, 108

Padroado, 42, 85f.
Pahlavi (middle Persian), 18f.
Pakistan, 134, 155-169 passim
Palamcottah, 61, 69f., 72, 95, 111
Panikkar, Raymond, 166f.
Panipat, 27
Paramahamsa, Rāmakrishna, 124
Paravas, 30, 33, 38, 52
Parliament, British, 65
Parsis, 73, 168
Patna, 86, 108, 117
Paul, K. T., 133, 144
Paul, R. D., 51n., 56n.
Pearson, Hugh, 58n., 59n., 60n.
Peking, 22, 41
Pennell, Theodore, 96
Penny, F., 51n.
Periah, Yerraguntla, 104
Persia, 18; Persian, 59
Peshawar, 77
Pfander, C. G., 80
Pickett, J. W., 105
Pillai, H. A. Krishna, 142
Plassey, battle of, 63
Plato, 14
Plütschau, Henry, 53
Pohle, 58
Polo, Marco, 21, 41
Pondicherry, 16, 43f., 53, 62, 63n., 85, 108f.
Poona, 144
Pope, The, 21, 30, 34f., 45, 48f., 85, 87, 109, 137
    Clement XIV, 45
    Gregory XVI, 86
    Leo XIII, 108f.
    Pius VII, 84
Pope, G. U., 25, 41

Popley, H. A., 133n.
Portugal, 32, 34, 42, 44, 48f.; king of, 30, 34, 42ff., 85; Portuguese, 16-52 passim, 82, 85, 108
Prayer Book, 70
pre-Dravidian people, 99, 103
Presbyterians, 149
Presidency College, Calcutta, 120
Propaganda (Sacred Congregation for the Propagation of the Faith), 42, 109
Protestants, 48-61 passim, 98, 109, 111, 145, 163; Protestant missions, 87
Pulicat, 52
Punjab, 17, 63, 76, 104, 130

Quetta, 96
Quilon, 16, 18, 20f., 23
Qur'ān, 159

Rajamundry, 136
Ramābai, Pandita, 95
Rāmakrishna Mission, 126
Ramnad, 40, 60
Ranaghat Medical Mission, 96
Raychaudhuri, H. C., 27n.
Reformation, The, 48, 152
Reinhardt, Walter, 85
Rewa, 112
Rhenius, Charles Theophilus Ewald, 70f.
Ricci, Matthew, 41
Rig Veda, 12f.
Ringeltaube, W. T., 71
Roche, Tiburtius, 137
Rockefeller Foundation, 97
Roe, Thomas, 50
Rogerius, Abraham, 52
Roman Catholics, 49-64 passim, 82, 84, 86, 98, 101, 110f., 145, 148, 150, 163; Roman Catholic Church (Roman Catholicism), 45, 53, 61, 81, 84ff., 101, 107, 137, 164; Roman Catholic missions, 38, 40f., 54, 86f., 102, 109

Roman Empire, 16, 18
Rome, 33, 36, 39, 42-45 *passim*, 82, 84, 108, 140, 164
Roy, Rāmmohun, 117-119 *passim*, 122
Roz, Francis, 36
Russia, 12

Salesians, The, 85
Salsette, 22
Salvation Army, 99
Samāj (of Keshub Chundar Sen), 121f.
Samru, Joanna Zebunissa, 85f.
Santal Mission of the Northern Churches, 101
Santals, 99f.
Sapor, Mar (Xabro), 20
Saracens (Muslims), 23
Sarasvati, Dayānand, 122ff.
Sardhana, 85f.
Sargent, Edward, 138
Sarma, D. S., 126n.
Satī, 66
Satyanathan, 61
Schwartz, Christian Friedrich, 58-61, 71
Scotland, 149; Church of, 72; Scots, The, 93
Scudder, Ida, 97
Scudder, John, 75
Scudders, The, 76, 95
Sefa, 22
Sen, Keshub Chunder, 120ff.
Sepoy Rising, 88
Serampore, 53, 67ff., 76, 80, 135f.; degree college founded, 69
Serfojee (Rajah), 60
Serra, 33, 35f.
Séverac, Jourdain Catalini de, 22; *see* Brother Jordan
Seward, Sara, 96
Shanars, 61, 71
Shar'iah, 159
Shāstra, 118
Sherring, M. A., 88n.
Sialkot, 104

Sikhs, 77
Siddhārtha, 14; *see* Buddha
Sierra Leone, 87
Simeon, Charles, 68
Sind, 63, 98
Singh, Māharāj, 164
Singh, Sādhu Sundar, 144
Skrefsrud, L. O., 101
smriti, 13
Somervell, T. H., 96
South India United Church, 148ff.
Spain, 49; Spaniards, 48
Spanish Carmelites, 36
sruti, 13
Stevens, Thomas (English Jesuit), 43
Stevenson, Mrs. Sinclair, 79
Sumer, 12
Sundkler, B. G. M., 148n.
Surat, 49, 79
Swain, Clara, 96
Syria, 106; Syriac, 19, 106; Syrians, 19f., 82f., 106, 111

Tagore, Debendranāth, 119
Tagore, Rabindranāth, 119, 132
Tambaram Conference, 143
Tanjore, 59f.
Taprobane, 18
Tatas, The, 93
Telugu, 38, 73, 98, 104
Terry, Edward, 50
Thangasamy, D. A., 143n.
Thoburn, Isabella, 95
Thomas, Apostle, 16ff., 21, 23, 34
Thomas Christians, 16, 21, 23f., 26, 33-36 *passim*, 47, 81, 88, 106, 108f., 150
Thomas, John, 71f., 86
Tibet, 41
Tilak, Nārāyan Vāman, 142
Tiruchendur, 33
Tirukurral, 25
Tirunelveli, 61, 69ff., 73, 136, 138f.
Tiruvalluvar, 25
Todas, 102f.
Tokat, 68